JANE'S
MILITARY REVIEW

edited by Ian V. Hogg

JANE'S
MILITARY REVIEW

edited by Ian V. Hogg

Sixth year of issue

JANE'S

First published in 1987 by
Jane's Publishing Company Limited
238 City Road, London EC1V 2PU

Distributed in the Philippines and
the USA and its dependencies by
Jane's Publishing Inc,
115 Fifth Avenue,
New York, NY 10003

ISBN 0 7106 0447 5

Typesetting by Method Limited
Epping, Essex

Printed in the United Kingdom by
Biddles Ltd, Guildford and King's Lynn

Publisher's note
The first compilation in this series, published in October
1981, was issued under the title *Jane's Military Annual
1981–82*.

Contents

Foreword

In this sixth edition of *Jane's Military Review* we have, as usual, covered a wide field of subjects of military interest. As always, we would stress that the views of the contributors are entirely their own and where these contributors hold official posts their views do not necessarily reflect those of their employers. The *Military Review* is a forum for opinions, and there is no restraint upon them.

We like, where possible, to try and look at different aspects of the military scene, not concentrating too much on one facet or another, and this year we have interesting analyses of two European armies, those of Eire and Spain, which are rarely in the news but which each have their own particular problems to face and their own solutions. After last year's discussion of the urban battle, we have a view of the same subject from a Territorial Army officer, and as a total contrast a close look at the Swedish coast defence system, an area which has never been revealed to the public before. Training is always of interest, and we have an overview of the impact of electronics on training, contrasting with an overview of the impact of training and other commitments on the available manpower of the British Army. Some current views on the value of mortars and the possibility of a return to the anti-tank and close support gun are aired, while the historically-minded reader is offered a little-known story of British wartime development, together with our usual light-hearted view of soldiering a century ago.

In addition to thanking the contributors for their endeavours, we must also thank Alex Vanags-Baginskis and the design staff of Jane's for their usual hard work in converting the raw material into a finished book.

The Military Year

Ian V. Hogg

When, early in 1985, the US Army selected the Beretta 92F as its new standard sidearm, we forecast that this would not be the end of the affair. Common sense and long experience of the wonders of military procurement made it fairly certain that those who had been unseated in the race would soon be at the steward's box voicing their objections. True to this prophecy, within weeks there were sufficient lawsuits to satisfy litigation freaks and ensure that the Cadillac Division of General Motors would not fall short of its sales target in the following year. In due course the sound and fury died away, but in June 1986 the Legislation and National Security Subcommittee of the US House of Representatives Committee on Government Operations held a hearing in Washington to consider the various aspects of the US Army's selection of the Beretta. In particular, the hearing was designed to consider the question of whether the Army's test procedure had accorded fair treatment to all the contestants.

As with all such committees, it is very hard, at the end of the day, to be sure of what sort of a decision it has come to, since its final conclusions are all ringed around with ifs, buts and maybes. On the whole, it does seem that one complaint was justified – that Smith & Wesson were wrongly eliminated in the firing-pin energy test, due to somebody doing his sums wrong in converting the NATO metric requirement into US dimensions.

But the other disputed area leaves us in some astonishment, not on technical grounds but on the grounds of what can be done to the English language when pressed. To quote the report, 'The request for test samples called for "an expected life of at least 5000 rounds". The word "expected" is defined in dictionary terms as "average" and is used in the same way as the phrase "life expectancy". The Army told firms that it needed pistols with an *average* service life of at least 5000 rounds ...'

With great respect to the honourable subcommittee, the Army said nothing of the sort; it said it expected to get 5000 rounds out of the pistol, and when the test pistol displayed a flaw at less than that figure, it rightly discarded it. What sort of dictionary equates 'expected' with 'average' defeats us. If the train is expected at 9 o'clock, one intends to get to the station at 8:59 and see it pulling in; the fact that it gets there any time between 8:55 and 9:05 is human failure, not a matter of semantics or of averages. One does not expect the railway company to set its timetables on the basis of the average performance of Driver Smith over three months.

The other interesting feature that emerges from this affair is the flexibility of the so-called 'NDI' concept. NDI means 'Non-Developmental Item' and is supposed to refer to equipment which can be bought off the shelf rather than be designed to meet some specific military requirement. Perhaps the easiest example would be an army requirement for a non-combat truck for doing the odd hauling jobs around the barracks. There is no need for it to meet a special list of requirements, and thus the Army can merely ask interested manufacturers what they have in the one-ton truck line, pick the one which suits it and is the cheapest, and buy it. No development required. To quote the report once more, 'The military wanted to select a commercial, off-the-shelf, non-developmental item that would replace the existing handguns ...' But the fact of the matter is that the Army laid down specifications which meant that there wasn't an off-the-shelf pistol in the world which would satisfy it, and the manufacturers spent large sums of money modifying existing pistols to meet the Army's demands. It may have been non-developmental so far as the Army were concerned, but it certainly wasn't so to the manufacturers. So perhaps NDI is in future to be construed as 'No-cost-to-us Developmental Item'.

Since writing the foregoing paragraphs, further moves have taken place. The 20 October edition of *Defense News* reported that 'The issue of a standard pistol for the armed forces, thought settled two years ago with the purchase of the 9 mm Beretta, has been reopened by a House–Senate compromise on the defense budget bill that orders the Army to conduct yet another handgun competition in 1987'. The compromise means that the existing five-year contract with Beretta will stand, but a fresh competition will now be held to decide which pistol will be adopted for subsequent purchase. Which blows the idea of standardisation straight into the weeds. This one will run and run.

However slipshod it may or may not have been over selecting a pistol, it would seem that the US Army does not intend to miss any chances in the development of its next rifle. It is anticipated that in another ten years or so the existing M16 rifle will be up for replacement, and for some years now the Army has been looking ahead and promoting its 'Advanced Combat Rifle Program'. About three years ago it gave contracts to Heckler & Koch and the AAI Corporation for the development of rifles firing caseless ammunition, and both companies have produced prototypes. Heckler & Koch, of course, have been occupied for the best part of 15 years in perfecting a caseless rifle for the Federal German Army, so by this time it has a fairly sound knowledge of what is what in this field. The AAI Corporation, perhaps less widely known, also has a long experience in the design of unusual firearms, but its caseless rifle appears to be a sound and workable weapon.

However, in order not to overlook any other possibility, in late-1986 further contracts were awarded to a number of companies: Steyr-Daimler Puch of Austria, McDonnell Douglas, the Ares Corporation and Colt Firearms. The Request for Proposals begins by saying that the army does not require a caseless solution, and invites 'alternative technology' instead. Due to a somewhat verbose opening commentary, the RFP was misread by a number of people, your editor included, to imply that the Army was no longer looking at caseless ammunition. In fact the Army is saying 'We already have two caseless solutions and we know all about caseless; what we want you to do is come up with some other brilliant idea, so that at the end of the day, and before we make a decision, we can at least be certain that every avenue has been thoroughly explored and no wildcat inventor will appear from behind a tree at the eleventh hour with something totally unexpected'.

This promises to be interesting. Who knows what bright ideas may be sitting around design offices, waiting to be translated into working models? Many years of talking with firearms' designers makes me feel fairly certain that there are several innovations which have never been followed up simply because of the expense involved. Few private firearms manufacturers have the financial resources to develop a bright but totally unconventional idea, because they know very well that even if they make it work, the amount of 'consumer resistance' to be overcome can quite easily defeat the end result, leaving them several millions out of pocket. Now a fairy godmother has appeared with a deep, not bottomless but deep enough, purse which will allow them to at least put together a 'technology demonstrator'. Even if, at the end of the day, the US Army says 'Thank you gentlemen, and please close the door as you leave', the participants will have got it out of their system at little or no expense to themselves and there may be some useful spin-off for the next generation of commercial firearms.

The past year has seen a surprising amount of information coming from China about new weapons; not weapons adopted by the People's Liberation Army, but weapons being offered on the open market, both military and commercial. Many of the designs appear to be little more than modifications of Soviet weapons, or, in some cases, resuscitations of older German designs, or even copies of Western models, but there are

Below: **A Chinese armoured personnel carrier mounting the Red Cloud 8 anti-tank missile system; the similarity with the French HOT and Milan turrets is apparent.**

Above: **Chinese 'Light Sub-machine Gun 7.62 mm Type 79'.**

Below: **Although on a ground mount, this is the Chinese '12.7 mm Anti-Aircraft Machine Gun Type 77'.**

evidences of original thought to be seen as well. Thus the 'Light Machine Pistol 9 mm' can be seen to be a direct copy of the Polish PM-63, the 'Semi-Automatic Sniping Rifle 7.62 mm' is a re-run of the Soviet Dragunov and the 'Type 56 Sub-Machine Gun' is the AK-47 Kalashnikov rifle with a folding bayonet beneath the barrel. The 'Machine Pistol Type 80' is the Mauser 712 *Schnellfeuerpistole* of the 1930s brought up to date, and the 'Pistol Type 77' is the even older Chylewski one-hand-cocking pistol rescued from oblivion, though to what purpose defeats me. The 'Anti-tank Weapon System Red Arrow 8' turns out to be a near-copy of the Anglo-French-German Milan wire-guided missile, though with some elements apparently taken from the American TOW missile system.

On the other hand the 'Light Sub-Machine Gun 7.62 mm Type 79' is a remarkable little weapon which is totally original. It fires the 7.62 mm pistol cartridge Type 51, which is the Soviet 7.62 mm pistol round, which, of course, is the Mauser 7.63 mm pistol round, an odd choice in many eyes but one which is adhered to by the Communists because of its penetration properties and because having a 7.62 mm sub-machine gun means standardisation of barrel-making machinery when the issue rifle is also 7.62 mm in calibre. The mechanism is

probably blowback, though there is an odd protrusion over the barrel which looks as if it ought to be some sort of gas cylinder but is probably clearance for a slightly overhung bolt and anchorage for a recoil spring guide. The barrel appears long and slender, there is a folding stock and the magazine holds 20 rounds. The illustrated brochure on the weapon is neither very forthcoming about its precise dimensions, nor about how it works, but perhaps these things will become clearer in due course; probably when the distributors actually put a weapon on display in the West instead of merely a pile of brochures.

Another original is the '12.7 mm Anti-Aircraft Machine Gun Type 77', the possibilities of which are fascinating several Western gun-watchers. It appears to be little more than a barrel with a thin tubular receiver behind it, and nobody is certain of just what the operating system is; and there certainly must be some breech locking system, for the weapon apparently weighs 56 kg with tripod and sights and it fires a hefty 12.7 mm cartridge at 800 metres per second.

As this is being written, 'Armdex 86' is being held in Peking; this is the first major arms exhibition to be held in China to which outside exhibitors and visitors have been invited, and it is anticipated that more information

11

about these (and other) new Chinese weapons will be released either at or in the wake of the show.

A report from Paris indicates that the French government are the first Europeans to shake off the anti-gas yoke. The French Foreign Minister confirmed, in November, that France intends to develop its own chemical weapons. Confronted by the fact of 'abundant and diversified stocks of chemical weapons in potential enemy countries', '... France cannot indefinitely renounce those categories of weapons which other nations consider they have the right to possess, or to accept seeing its defence troops paralysed by an aggressor should it decide to use chemical weapons'.

Hitherto the French riposte to a chemical attack would have been to 'go nuclear', but it has now been realised that it would be highly unlikely that any French president would accept the odium of initiating nuclear warfare, whatever the provocation, and that the only sensible response to chemical warfare is chemical warfare.

It will be interesting to see what the result to this will be. France and NATO have a curious relationship, and it may well be that the Warsaw Pact will choose to consider this as a solely French decision and take little notice. On the other hand it is likely that it will be seen as a quasi-NATO decision, in which case we can look forward to a massive propaganda effort to mobilise 'Public Opinion' against the idea. Forget cruise missiles, forget neutron bombs, gas will be the flavour of 1987 for the 'Agitprop Rentamob'. Porton Down and Nancekuke will again be visited by the travelling objectors, investigative television reporters will hint at mysterious factories and suspicious illnesses, and the usual signatures will appear on petitions and manifestos.

The past few months have seen correspondence in the newspapers about racial bias in the British Army. Apparently the proportion of coloured people in the United Kingdom is not reflected in the proportion of coloured people in Her Majesty's Forces. A point which few people appear to have appreciated is that Her Majesty's Forces are volunteers, and hence the percentages are never likely to balance unless we can have some assurance from the experts that an equal percentage of coloured people are actually reporting to the recruiting offices. You could equally say that the Army's percentage of plumbers or barristers or red-haired men six feet tall is not representative of the national ratio. How do we know what drives plumbers or barristers or red-haired men to volunteer or stay away? How do we know what coloured people think about volunteering? In my experience, which is considerable, men enlist for all sorts of reasons, and they doubtless choose not to enlist for as many more reasons. The only way to ensure the correct proportions of all the possible variants - coloured, Mormon, Jewish, Welsh, red-haired or whatever - would be to introduce universal conscription, and we know how popular that would be with the people who are making the present objections.

From time to time throughout the past twelve months the newspapers have given information on the on-again-off-again story of the privatisation of the Royal Ordnance Factories. I do not propose to go over this ground again, for I am far from certain that I have understood all the shifts and changes. But apropos of this question of privatisation, I will tell two stories.

The first took place in August 1940, when sub-machine guns were desperately needed for the defence of Britain. Several designs were being examined and tested, and in the course of these tests it was found that British-manufactured 9 mm Parabellum ammunition 'was inclined to fire auto when set for single shot'. At that time the production of 9 mm ammunition was virtually non-existent in Britain, and the small pre-war manufacture had been for pistols. Messrs XYZ, the makers of the ammunition in question, were sent a Beretta sub-machine gun and some Italian ammunition and asked if they could produce cartridges which would work effectively.

'We have no doubt we can supply satisfactory ammunition after some further experimental work, but we do not propose to do anything further unless an order is placed with us. In the meantime, we get over the trouble by having the cases slightly oily; it is sufficient to rub the cartridges with an oily rag.

(We then received) a letter from CIA Woolwich stating he understands that the incorrect functioning ... might be overcome by hardening the head of the case and thereby saving oiling. He also asked us for 200 of these improved rounds.

We think that our position is not quite clear to you. By an order we naturally meant something of the order of 25,000 to 50,000, since it is very uneconomical to alter machines from their present work to make 200 9 mm Parabellum ... It should be understood that if we are required to produce ... 9 mm Parabellum, it will be at the expense of .455 revolver.'

On reviewing this correspondence, the Ordnance Board commented:

'The Board have referred on several occasions to the extremely unsatisfactory nature of the work of Messrs XYZ, more particularly since the beginning of the war. Not only is the quality of their products poor but their attitude towards attempts to improve them is unhelpful ... It is therefore strongly recommended that one of the new factories should be set up to manufacture this ammunition and that no reliance be placed on Messrs XYZ ...'

And that was what happened; the Royal Ordnance Factory, Hirwaun, in South Wales, spent the entire war turning out millions of 9 mm Parabellum cartridges.

The second story concerns Naval armour-piercing shells. It will be recalled that the Navy complained about its shells as long ago as the Battle of Jutland, and in 1940, after the Battle of the River Plate, examination of the wreck of the *Admiral Graf Spee* showed that the current naval armour piercing shells were not up to the mark either. In January 1940 the Ordnance Board received a report on the testing of some naval AP shells against armour plate, and the results were not good:

'This is the first of a new series of (armour) plates. The two shell failures, particularly that of the 15-inch at 1900 ft/sec, are disquieting. The Board are of the opinion that the time has come for a thorough investigation of the allied questions of armour plate and piercing shell manufacture . . .'

Ten days later, Messrs ABC requested facilities for testing two shells 'in order to investigate some manufacturing improvements they have made'.

'The Board note with satisfaction that Messrs ABC have come to the conclusion that their methods of manufacturing AP shell require reviewing. They recommend that this opportunity be taken to put an end to the present individual system of investigation in which each of the shell-making firms carries out its own series of inadequate trials and keeps secret most of the data necessary for an intelligent appreciation of the results.

The Board do not question the zeal and ability of the men who are responsible for the manufacture; but they are convinced that no men, however able, can get the best results from the out-of-date system which now prevails . . .

When research is conducted, year after year, behind closed doors, it gets into a rut and, even if the workers have exceptionally high ability, does not produce the results which would be expected from work which is open to the comments and suggestions of other experts. It is a direct consequence of this secretive system that there is still no one in a position to correlate the results of all the costly trials that have been carried out the AP shell in the past . . . because the Board have been unable to obtain, until recently, details concerning the physical properties of the plates at which the shells have been fired and are still unable to obtain details of the composition and heat treatment of the shell. If it is to be ensured that HM Ships are supplied with the highest quality and best design of AP shell that it is possible to produce, all those who have knowledge of the subject must pool what they know, and it must be decided on what lines and on what scale trials are to be carried out.

The Board recommend, therefore, that Messrs ABC be discouraged from firing the small trial they propose, and that they and Messrs DEF and GHI should be asked to disclose any secret knowledge they may have and discuss with service representatives how best to apply what is now known and what trials should be staged to investigate the unknown. The investigation of what is causing some of our heavy piercing shell to fail has already been postponed too long . . .'

How much ice this appeal cut can be gauged from a report, made in the following month, by an inspector who had gone to Messrs ABC to discuss their instructing other firms of the manufacturing techniques for 2-pounder anti-tank shot, so as to speed up supply. They eventually agreed to supply tempering furnaces to other firms, but refused to supply drawings, preferring to build and supply the furnaces themselves.

'While Messrs ABC are willing to assist by showing a representative from each firm around their heat treatment plant, they desire these visits to be limited. Their responsibility ends with their having placed at our disposal the information contained in the notes drafted by us after our visit, the terms of reference of which covered only the heat treatment of 2-pr shot. The firm was not prepared to supply details of the steel making, rolling and forging practice adopted by them in the manufacture of this munition.'

One might think that the parlous state in which Britain found itself in the latter part of 1940 might have spurred these (and other) companies to sink their differences and co-operate to the utmost so as to produce the arms and munitions so desperately needed. Not a bit of it. The bickering over the relevation of trade secrets of the manufacture of heavy naval shells went on until 1944 when, in exasperation, the Ordnance Board set up the Royal Ordnance Factory, Cardonald, to manufacture the required shells 'in-house'. The old firms were scornful, but in fact the ROF was producing high quality shells before the war was over. Even then the old firms scoffed; there is a classic example of statistical analysis which came after a trial of the first two 15-inch Cardonald AP shells, which were fired in comparison with two other similar shells made by two of the old firms. One Cardonald shell failed to pierce the target plate, as did one of the competing shells. The representative of Messrs XYZ, at the subsequent meeting, is reported to have said 'Told you they couldn't do it; look at the result. Only one of our shells failed, but fifty per cent of their production was rubbish.'

Forty-five years ago the Ordnance Board found it necessary to take armaments manufacture out of the hands of private companies and put it into Royal Ordnance Factories. Now other heads, far less wise in the ways of munitions, propose to reverse the whole procedure. *Verbum sapienti sat est*. Or is it?

Hansard, 17 November 1986:

Mr McNamara asked the Secretary of State for Defence what has been the cost of the SP70 project to date.

Mr Archie Hamilton: The estimated cost of UK participation in the SP70 trinational development programme to date has been some £88 million.

Mr McNamara asked the Secretary of State if Britain intends to withdraw from the SP70 programme.

Mr Archie Hamilton: Ministers are reviewing the way ahead on the SP70 programme in the light of recommendations from national arms directors. It is hoped to reach decisions as soon as possible.

Two years ago, attending a military exercise in Germany, I asked a British gunner about SP70; he curled his lip and replied, 'Don't you mean SP2000?' This equipment has been under development for the past 14 years. Two prototypes were tried in Sardinia in 1979; ten more, of varying configuration, have been built and subjected to innumerable tests and trials since then. And we are still no nearer to seeing the equipment in service than we were in 1973.

The French Army required a 155 mm SP howitzer and began its development in 1969; it went into production in 1977. OTO Melara of Italy began developing its own design (SP155) in 1977 and put it into production in 1982. Spain and Taiwan have also developed their own designs, and there is a long list of people who have taken the existing American 155 mm howitzer barrel and mounted it on vehicles of their own design. The counter-argument is that, of course, the SP70 will be a high-technology design with automatic loading, very sophisticated sights and fire control, et cetera, et cetera. But the French GCT155 has a highly efficient automatic loading system, a firing system better than anything the SP70 is likely to use, and sights and fire control which it would be hard to fault. I have had the opportunity to climb all over the GCT155, to examine it thoroughly and watch it working, and I have also seen some of the high-technology aspects of SP70, particularly the automated loading mechanism, and there is no doubt in my mind as to who has got it right. To be blunt, the loading mechanism on the SP70 was, when I saw it, a plumber's nightmare, with no more application to a service equipment than a grand piano would be.

Why should this be? Are we seeing yet another example of Watson-Watt's Law 'The Best is the Enemy of the Good'? Is it because (as I suspect) no practical artilleryman was ever allowed near SP70 during the design phase and the engineers and scientists have had a field day? Is there in-fighting between the three national design teams? Have the Italians drilled holes in the wrong place so that the British bolts won't go through the holes in the German bits? To take 14 years over something as relatively simple as a self-propelled howitzer is a scandal, and the design teams should be ashamed of their ineptitude.

Since the lines above were written, the SP70 project has been terminated. On 13 January 1987 it was announced that the trinational development was to end and that 'each country would seek their own solution'. It was also disclosed that the abortive programme has cost Britain £88 million, and one can only suppose it has cost the other two partners similar amounts. Since that date further disclosures have shown that there were serious problems with the turret training mechanism which prevented the gun from being aimed accurately. In a perfect world none of this would have happened; in a near-perfect world those responsible would be fired; but in the real world in which we exist, it is probable that those responsible will now be shifted to other programmes where they can once more demonstrate their incompetence at the public expense.

The Irish Republic – Odd Man Out of European Defence

Adrian J. English

Occupying a geographical position relative to Western Europe analogous to that of Cuba to the Americas, Ireland has an obvious strategic significance, both in the context of NATO and the EEC. Although a committed member of the latter, the Republic of Ireland, which accounts for 80 per cent of the area of the island, is the only member state of the EEC which is not also a member of NATO and in fact professes a neutrality which it is only indifferently equipped to maintain. As the European Community becomes progressively a political as well as an economic grouping, the Republic may be faced with a difficult choice between its neutrality and demands to participate in the defence of the community.

Historical Background

The Anglo-Irish Treaty of 1921 established the 26 counties of southern Ireland as the Irish Free State, a Dominion within the British Commonwealth of Nations. Six of the nine counties of Ulster, the country's northern province, remained part of the United Kingdom, although enjoying a measure of regional autonomy, with a Parliament responsible for purely domestic affairs. Naval defence of the entire island however, remained an Imperial responsibility, the Royal Navy retaining bases at Queenstown (now renamed Cobh) in Cork harbour, at Berehaven, on the south coast of the Free State and at Lough Swilly, in the north-west. Britain also remained responsible for the extensive coastal defences of these installations, which continued to be manned by the British Army.

Despite the worsening international situation, an agreement was negotiated between the British and Irish Free State governments in 1938 whereby the so-called 'Treaty Ports' were handed over to the southern Irish government. When war broke out between Britain and Germany the following year, the Irish Free State chose to remain neutral, the only member state of the British Commonwealth to do so.

Although militarily weak, the Irish Free State, now known as Eire, managed to maintain its neutrality throughout the Second World War. German plans for the invasion of Ireland came to naught because of the lack of physical means to implement them and to sustain an invading force once a beach-head was established. The Allies, who also considered invasion, were dissuaded from doing so by political considerations which outweighed the probable advantage of access to southern Irish bases.

The successful maintenance of a neutrality which might have been more accurately described as 'non-belligerence' converted a concept which was but dimly understood by the bulk of the Irish people and many of their political leaders into the basis of Irish foreign policy. When the North Atlantic Treaty Organisation was set up in 1949, Eire, which had almost simultaneously severed its last political links with Britain when it declared itself the Republic of Ireland, declined an invitation to participate on the grounds that NATO bound its members to respect their existing frontiers, an undertaking which was considered incompatible with the aspiration to sovereignty over the entire island expressed in Articles 2 and 3 of the Irish Constitution. That countries with frontier disputes dating back, at least in the case of Greece and Turkey, to remote pre-history, found NATO membership acceptable left successive Irish governments unimpressed, although a proposal for a bilateral defence treaty between Ireland and the United States, following the outbreak of the Korean War, was rejected by the latter country.

Despite professing adherence to the principles and values which the North Atlantic Treaty Organisation was intended to defend, any suggestion of participation in NATO became as emotive an issue as the continuing partition of the island. Accession to full membership of the European Economic Community in 1973 failed to bring about any change in Irish defence policy although subsequent to joining the Community it was repeatedly stated by Irish political leaders that the Republic was prepared to participate in the defence of the Community if called upon to do so. Such protestations notwith-standing, the few occasions when Irish EEC delegates have been called upon to participate in discussions even peripherally related to defence matters have occasioned something approaching panic on the home front as have the more recent relevations of frequent overflights of Irish territory by NATO aircraft, the intrusions of NATO submarines into Irish territorial waters and (unsubstantiated) allegations that Irish telecommuni-cations equipment played some (unspecified) role in the NATO military communications network. The ap-parently almost universal antipathy towards NATO by politicians of both right and left is the more remarkable in the context of the widespread popular and official indifference to the incursions of Soviet aircraft and submarines into Ireland's air space and territorial waters.

The rights and duties of neutral powers are defined under the Hague Convention of 1907 which forms the major basis for the establishment of neutral status under international law. Under this Convention it is apparent that a simple declaration of neutrality is not sufficient to establish neutral status. Neutral states must take whatever military measures are necessary to ensure that their territory is not used in any way by one belligerent to the disadvantage of another. Those which fail to comply with this provision may lose their neutral status and a belligerent may take whatever military or political action is necessary to ensure that the territory of a non-belligerent is not used to its own military disadvantage.

The classic examples of the implementation of an effective policy of armed neutrality are Sweden and Switzerland, both of which maintain 'relatively impressive military establishments at very considerable expense both in human and economic terms. Both of these countries maintain armed forces which are not only adequate to comply with their obligations as neutrals under the Hague Convention but also offer very real military deterrence to a possible aggressor. Among other ostensible neutrals, Austria and Finland,

both of which have had neutrality forced upon them as the price of their continued independent existence, although spending proportionately less on defence than the two major traditional European neutrals, have each taken adequate measures within their respective resources to enforce their neutrality according to the terms of the Convention.

The Irish Military Establishment

The Irish Republic has always maintained a military establishment which is both inconsistent with its strategic importance and inadequate to enforce its neutrality during a conflict in which it was not involved. Although an armed force of some 50,000 was maintained throughout most of the Second World War, its equipment, in particular that of its naval and air elements, was never adequate either to deter an aggressor or even to enforce its declared neutrality on any realistic level and the country remained dependent on external sources of supply for even such elementary items as small arms ammunition.

Following the return of peace, the personnel establishment of the defence forces was reduced to 13,000, including a small Naval Service and Air Corps, the Army being organised into three infantry brigades, with no heavy armour or artillery. From 1959 to 1979 the regular Army was further diluted by theoretical integration with the part-time territorial defence force to provide six largely mythical brigades. In 1979 this arrangement was replaced by a more rational one in which regular Army elements were to provide a manoeuvre force of four brigades, local defence becoming logically the responsibility of the territorial defence force.

Almost continuous participation in United Nations peace-keeping operations since the early 1960s, together with the threat of an overspill of violence from Northern Ireland from 1969 onwards, had also brought about some improvement in the equipment situation of the Army and a 40 per cent increase in its effectives while EEC membership and responsibility for policing a 136,000 sq mile (352,000 km²) exclusive Economic Zone had also occasioned some expansion and re-equipment of the Navy and Air Corps.

The Irish Defence Forces in the 1980s.

The Irish defence forces remain a single tri-service entity in which the Naval Service and Air Corps form integral parts, although the Navy expresses its functional individuality by possessing distinctive uniforms and rank structure. The current establishment of the permanent defence force is 17,957 all ranks, with a strength of 13,941 at the end of July 1986. Recruitment is entirely voluntary and defence expenditure for the year 1986–87 was estimated at approximately US $340 million, of which pay accounted for approximately 70 per cent, capital expenditure on new equipment amounting to an unimpressive US $7 million.

The Army, with an establishment of 15,453 and an actual strength of 12,181, consists of 11 infantry battalions (plus an additional *ad hoc* battalion group serving with UNIFIL); two independent infantry companies; a special forces unit; one light tank squadron; four armoured cavalry squadrons; three field artillery regiments; one air defence regiment and three combat engineer companies, plus logistic support units.

These are deployed between four territorial Commands of which the most important is Eastern Command (HQ Dublin), with a single infantry brigade consisting of two infantry battalions, an armoured cavalry squadron, an artillery regiment, a combat engineer company and support units, all stationed at the capital, plus an infantry force (essentially a two-battalion brigade, without combat support units) deployed along the eastern portion of the border with Northern Ireland, the two independent infantry companies and various non-combatant support units being stationed at Dublin.

Second in importance and largest in area is Western Command (HQ Athlone), with a brigade of identical composition to that in the Eastern Command, but with the addition of a third attached infantry battalion employed on border security. Southern Command (HQ Cork), also has a two-battalion brigade, with identical support units to those in the Eastern and Western Commands as its manoeuvre element while Curragh Command, with its HQ at the enormous but rather down-at-heel military complex of Curragh Camp, some 30 miles to the south-west of Dublin and inherited from the British, covers the south-eastern part of the country with a fourth two-battalion brigade, in this case supported only by an armoured cavalry squadron. This Command also normally accommodates the special forces unit, the tank squadron and the sole regular battery of the air defence regiment, in addition to the Military College and most of the Army's training establishments.

Below: **Irish Army patrol on the Republic/Northern Ireland Border. The infantryman beside the radio-equipped Land-Rover carries a Swedish Carl-Gustav KPist 45 sub-machine gun, the standard light automatic weapon of the Irish Defence Forces.**

Left: **Dismounted cavalrymen with FN MAG machine gun which is used in the light and medium roles by the Irish Army. The French AFV crewmen's helmet distinguishes them from other arms who until recently used the British M.1944 pattern. Since mid-1985 both types have been superseded by fibreglass ballistic helmets of Israeli design.**

Below left: **Infantry with Hotchkiss-Brandt 81 mm mortar. The vehicle behind the wall is a Panhard AML 245 armoured car.**

Below: **Panhard AML VTT M3, the Irish Army's standard armoured personnel carrier. In theory each infantry battalion has an APC mounted rifle company although in practice only the 3rd, stationed at the Curragh Camp, Co. Kildare, the 5th, at Dublin and the 27th, 28th and 29th, deployed on the Border between the Republic and Northern Ireland, have their full allocation of vehicles. Each cavalry squadron also has an APC mounted troop.**

Backing this force is the part-time Territorial Reserve, with an establishment of 22,214; the 15,171 enrolled members manning 18 infantry battalions, three motorised cavalry squadrons, six field artillery regiments, three air defence batteries, three combat engineer companies and logistic support units. Of these, four infantry battalions, a motorised cavalry squadron, a field artillery regiment, an air defence battery and a combat engineer company provide the territorial defence element of Eastern Command. Western and Southern Commands each have six infantry battalions, a motorised cavalry squadron, two artillery regiments and an engineer company. Southern Command also has two air defence batteries, while Curragh Command has only two infantry battalions and an artillery regiment.

The regular infantry are equipped with the 7.62 mm calibre FN FAL rifle (various potential replacements in 5.56 mm calibre being currently under active consideration although these are unlikely to be adopted in the forseeable future in view of prevailing economic circumstances), the 9 mm Carl Gustav M45 submachine gun, the 7.62 mm MAG general-purpose machine gun and the 0.50-in (12.7 mm) calibre Browning M2HB heavy machine gun. The principal

Below: **Members of the 1st Tank Squadron with the Scorpion light tank, the only tracked AFV operated by the Irish Army.**

support weapons are 60 mm and 81 mm Hotchkiss-Brandt mortars, the 84 mm Carl Gustav M2 rocket launcher and the 90 mm Bofors 1110 RCL. Four Milan ATGW firing posts are used for training but the project to equip at least the regular infantry battalions with this weapon has also been a victim of economic cuts. The special forces are equipped primarily with the 5.56 mm HK-33 assault rifle and the HK-53 sub-machine gun.

The volunteer reservists are still primarily equipped with the old Lee-Enfield No 4 rifle and the Bren and Vickers machine guns, all in 0.303-in calibre, the more

Right: **A Panhard H-60 armoured car of which the Irish Army operates a total of 32. This vehicle belongs to the first batch of 16 acquired and is armed with the HB-60 breech-loading mortar. Various projects to rearm these vehicles exist but have been the victims of economies in defence spending. The 16 more recently delivered vehicles are armed with the Thompson-Brandt 60 mm LR gun-mortar.**

modern support weapons being issued on a reduced scale to that applying to regular units. It is also unlikely that they will inherit many of the FAL rifles when the regular infantry re-equips on 5.56 mm calibre as the majority of these weapons are almost worn out after 25 years of service.

Armour consists of 14 Scorpion light tanks, 20 AML H-90 and 32 H-60 armoured cars, plus 60 AML-VTT and ten locally-built Timoney APCs. Several projects exist for up-gunning the Panhard H-60 armoured cars

Below: **A Panhard H-90 armoured car of the Irish Army's 1st Armoured Squadron. This is the most formidable AFV operated by the Irish Army, each cavalry squadron having a support troop of four. UN service infantry battalions also incorporate four H-90s and 13 Panhard APCs in their reconnaissance companies.**

Left: **Members of the 2nd Field Artillery Regiment with the elderly British 25 pounder gun-howitzer which still equips two regular and six reserve field batteries. Of two batteries of 105 mm Light Guns delivered, one is operated by the 3rd Field Battery, which serves both as the sole artillery support element of the 6th brigade and as a demonstration unit for the Artillery School at Kildare; the other forms part of the 4th Field Artillery Regiment. The remaining batteries use the Brandt 120 mm heavy mortar in the artillery role.**

Below left: **Irish Army Engineers erecting a Fairey Medium Girder Bridge.**

Below: **Lt Gen Callaghan, senior officer of the Irish Defence Forces and currently on semi-permanent secondment to the United Nations as Chief of Staff of the United Nations Truce Supervisory Organization in the Middle East, having commanded the United Nations Interim Force in Lebanon from 1981 to 1986, inspects a naval guard of honour. Although forming an integral part of the Defence Forces, the Irish Naval Service expresses its individuality by different uniforms and rank structure. The naval rating's uniform combines British, French and German elements although the uniforms of officers and petty officers closely resemble those of the Royal Navy, apart from rank insignia, which follows US practice. Army uniforms and insignia are almost identical to those of their British counterparts.**

but financial constraints render their implementation problematic in the foreseeable future.

The programme to re-equip at least the regular field artillery elements with the British 105 mm light gun has been another victim of economic cutbacks after only two six-gun batteries had been delivered, the only other field artillery pieces in service being 48 25-pounder gun-howitzers of Second World War vintage, plus 72 120 mm Brandt mortars used in the artillery role.

The air defence elements are equipped with 24 elderly 40 mm L/60 Bofors AA guns, with a pair of L/70s being used for training as are seven RBS-70 SAM firing posts. The four air defence batteries, each of which in theory consists of one troup of guns and one of missiles, are therefore equipped only to half of their nominal establishments and with obsolescent material.

Left: **The helicopter-carrying OPV *Eithne*, currently the largest unit of the Irish Naval Service.**

Above: **The OPV *Aisling*, the most recently completed of three vessels of the 'P 22' class. Both these, the slightly smaller *Deirdre*, and the *Eithne*, are locally designed and built.**

Communications and motor transport equipment is likewise largely obsolescent, many vehicles being over 20 years old.

For an island country, the Republic maintains an extremely modest naval force.

The establishment of the Naval Service is 1277 all ranks, actual strength being 930. *L. E. Eithne*, the only one to be built of two helicopter-carrying frigate-type offshore patrol vessels of approximately 2000 tons full-load displacement, the construction of which was projected in the mid-1970s, is currently its largest unit. Although designed as a naval vessel she carries only a very light armament, consisting of a single 57 mm Bofors Mk I dual-purpose and two 20 mm Rheinmetall AA guns, plus an embarked SA.365F Dauphin helicopter. There are also three 'P 22' class OPVs of about 1000 tons, each armed with one 40 mm L/60 Bofors and two 20 mm Oerlikon AA guns, plus a similar but slightly smaller vessel. Two ex-British 'Ton' class coastal minesweepers (a third sister-ship was disposed of in 1984) are laid up and unlikely to go to sea again. Tentative plans for their replacement by a similar number of minesweeper/hunters of the Netherlands 'Alkmaar' class are not likely to be realised in the present economic climate, even though the EEC pays 50 per cent of the capital cost of equipment for policing Ireland's 136,000 sq mile (352,000 km²) share of the Community's Exclusive Economic Zone. Two to four patrol vessels of the French 'P400' class may however be acquired in the forseeable future for this purpose.

The Navy itself estimates that a total of 12 vessels is the minimum necessary for effective peace-time Economic Zone policing but the likelihood of expanding the fleet to even this modest size seems remote. The possibility of the acquisition of vessels with a serious combat capability remains in the realm of fantasy.

Above: **The minesweeper *Grainne*, like her sisters *Banba* and *Fola*, former members of the British 'Ton' class. The two surviving vessels are decommissioned and unlikely to go to sea again, leaving the Irish Navy with no mine counter-measures capacity.**

The old Royal Naval base at Haulbowline Island, Cobh, remains the only shore establishment, apart from a small naval presence at defence forces' HQ in Dublin, although recruit training is carried out, on a temporary basis, at an army camp near Cork. The Naval Service also includes a small volunteer reserve element, organised in five companies who train largely in pulling whalers, with a week at sea each year in the Service's diminishing number of sea-going vessels. A small sail training ship, built for the Navy, has been judged to be employed to better political advantage in connection with civilian youth training schemes and is so used, although still owned by the Department of Defence.

The situation of the Air Corps also leaves much to be desired. This force has an establishment of 1227 but an actual strength of only 830 all ranks with 42 aircraft, divided between three operational wings and eight nominal squadrons. Of these, six Fouga CM.170 Super Magister and nine SIAI Marchetti SF.260W trainers have a limited ground-support/light strike capability, as do eight Reims-Cessna F-172H and K liaison aircraft and all elements of the helicopter force. This comprises five recently delivered SA.365F Dauphins, two SA.342 Gazelles and eight SA.316 Alouette IIIs. Two Beech Super King Air 200s serve in the maritime patrol role, a third aircraft of this type being used to back up the single

HS-125 which is primarily used to ferry various VIPs between Dublin, Brussels and Luxemburg. The lack of equipment with even a nominal capacity to impede incursions into Irish air space is especially notable.

The replacement of the Super King Airs used for maritime patrol is becoming critical, because these aircraft, designed for the light transport role, have become heavily corroded after nearly ten years of low-altitude flying in marine atmospheres.

Modest expansion plans, which include the acquisition of a dozen or so BAe Hawk aircraft, for the fighter/light strike role, three SA.330 Super Puma transport helicopters and two additional Gazelles, plus five SIAI Marchetti SF.260C fixed-wing trainers and the ultimate replacement of the Alouettes by a similar number of Dauphins, seem most unlikely to be realised in the foreseeable future, a single Super Puma, which

Top right: **A Reims-Cessna 172H aircraft of the Army Co-operation Squadron of the Irish Air Corps, configured for the ground-support role.**

Centre right: **An SIAI Marchetti SF 260W training aircraft of the Irish Air Corps. These aircraft, like the Fouga CM.170-2 Super Magisters also operated in the training role have a limited light strike capability but the force lacks true combat aircraft.**

Right: **One of two SA.365F helicopters operated in the maritime support role by the Irish Air Corps, here shown on the flight deck of the OPV *Eithne*, the only vessel of the Irish Naval Service equipped to handle aircraft. Three similar aircraft serve in the SAR role.**

was operated on lease between 1981 and 1983, having been returned as a economy measure shortly after proving its usefulness for disaster relief during the unusually harsh winter of 1982–83.

The Air Corps operates two permanent bases: at Baldonnel, Co. Dublin and Gormanston, Co. Meath, and maintains helicopter flight elements on detachment to two of the Army's three border infantry battalions but has no volunteer reserve element.

Summary and Prospects

As will be seen from the foregoing, although the Defence Forces of the Republic are currently better equipped than at any time in their 65-year history, their equipment is largely orientated towards the internal security role. The Army has effectively become a gendarmerie and the Navy a coast-guard/fishery protection force, with a small air arm barely sufficient for the support of the land and sea elements in their respective very limited current roles. Although their personnel are exceptionally well-trained and motivated, particularly in the context of a consistent policy of official neglect, morale is rapidly being eroded by current economic stringency, manifested not only in the effective abandonment of all re-equipment programmes but also in an embargo on recruiting which results in a cumulative annual decrease in strength, with no corresponding reduction in largely distasteful non-military commitments, such as cash escorts and prison guard duties. A 50 per cent reduction in the annual two-week training period of the volunteer reserves, as part of the economy programme, must also diminish the potential of these elements.

The lack of any significant military capability is painfully obvious, the explicit intention of converting the four regular brigades into mechanised units, each presumably with one armoured and two APC-mounted infantry battalions, announced in 1979, has not materialised while the provision of combat equipment for the Naval Service and Air Corps has not received even official lip-service.

To provide a credible deterrent to the violation of its neutrality, on a comparable basis to the smaller neutral European states, the Republic would need to engage in an expansion and re-equipment programme for its defence forces involving a capital expenditure of over US $650 million or nearly twice its current annual defence spending.

To maintain the above would cost somewhere between US $700 million and 1.5 billion annually or between twice and four times current expenditure, which at 1.5 per cent of GNP is already equivalent to the proportion of national wealth spent on defence by such small neutral states as Austria or Finland, while Sweden or the smaller NATO powers such as Belgium, Norway and Denmark spend approximately twice as much. As Ireland is currently the second most highly taxed country in the EEC, with revenue accounting for almost 40 per cent of GNP, further expenditure to support a realistic defence policy would be neither practical nor politically feasible.

The Republic is fortunate that the *Pax Atomica* has diminished its apparent strategic importance in the context of Mutually Assured Destruction in the case of war between East and West, the only serious conflict scenario likely to threaten its territorial integrity. In this context it has been able to indulge in what has with some justice been termed 'parasitic neutrality', trusting implicitly to the NATO umbrella for its external defence while still declining to make any contribution to that umbrella. However, the Strategic Defence Initiative, if it gets off the ground, by largely neutralising the threat of immediate Armageddon in the event of a major clash between the Eastern and Western military blocs, may reopen the possibility of a war between these blocs fought with conventional weapons. This possibility also further opens up the likelihood of an intensification of the hitherto tentative efforts which have been made to involve the Republic in Community defence, something not necessarily synonymous with NATO. In that case a country which has hitherto been happy to accept fairly considerable EEC financial assistance in the development of both its naval and air defence forces, without any reciprocal commitment to its benefactors, may find itself in the difficult position of either providing such commitment or withdrawing from the Community, with all the economic implications of such a move. If this situation should develop, the political dilemma of the government of the day will be particularly unenviable, the myth of neutrality having been apparently so effectively sold to the Irish public that, according to a recent survey, 86 per cent of the Republic's population actively support its retention as the keystone of national foreign policy.

Battlefield Evolution and the Third Dimension

Bryan Perrett

When, in 1580, the Frenchman Philip de Commines wrote that 'The English are the flowers of the archers of the world', he spoke no more than the truth, for they practised with their longbows from childhood, drawing to the ear with a pull-weight of not less than 40 and sometimes 80 kg, shooting up to twelve 760 mm-long shafts per minute with frightening accuracy, and the penetrative power concentrated in the narrow heads of their arrows had become legendary. Many toxophilites claim, with some justice, that the longbow would have provided the British infantry at Waterloo with a better weapon than the musket, and that the same was true as late as the Crimean War.

Thirty-five years before Commines paid his hereditary enemies his sincere compliment, Henry VIII's favourite warship, the *Mary Rose*, capsized and sank off Portsmouth in action against the French, taking with her all but a tiny handful of her company. This included a reinforced contingent of archers, a large number of whose weapons have been recovered and carefully preserved. Also salvaged were many of the ship's guns but there is little doubt that these weapons were still regarded by some of the bowmen aboard as being just as dangerous to friend as to foe, while their masters, the professional gunners, were clearly damned for all eternity by their attempts to expand technology beyond the limits wisely set by the Almighty. The presence of several breech-loaders was probably as welcome as the arrival of a rabid primate in a nuclear power station, for the 'breech' was merely an ingot dropped into place behind the barrel and, as the old hands would mutter darkly, the back-blast of gases was so great that sooner or later it would blow out, taking a few heads with it.

Of course, it was the gunners who were on the right lines and it needed only the passage of time and improved technology to prove the point. The majority of weapon systems are naturally primitive when first conceived, but with perseverence they evolve. The application of the available technology, coupled with tactical and strategic flexibility, has always been the hallmark of good generalship. Thus, the Macedonians were quick to realise that a concentration of big men with long spears was more than a match for a similar concentration of average-sized men with shorter spears. The answer to the Macedonian phalanx was the tactical flexibility of the Roman legion, which was able to carve its way into the flank of the mass with its short swords. The infantry-heavy legion, however, was terribly vulnerable to the firepower and mobility of the Parthians' mounted bowmen. At Hastings the apparently unbreakable Saxon shield-wall was eventually smashed by a combination of firepower and shock action. As the Middle Ages progressed the former element was neglected and chivalry chose to rely on shock action unaided to attain its object until, quite literally, it was stopped in its tracks by the longbow, providing one of the rare periods in history when the power of the defence exceeded that of the attack. The firearm replaced the bow, the bayonet the pike and body armour was abandoned, but for the next three centuries further technical, and therefore tactical, development was slow. Then improved industrial processes led to the drawn brass cartridge case, leading to quick-firing artillery and automatic weapons. By 1914 these, together with barbed wire, had again given the defence greater power than the attack, so that fighting quickly degenerated into virtual siege warfare. Recognising that only the restoration of mobility could produce a decisive result, every army sought to break the stalemate, the British and French with the tank, the Germans with storm troop battalions trained for infiltration and deep penetration. The result was that the battles of 1918 possessed a degree of movement which had been lacking in the previous three years.

What might have happened had the First World War continued was forecast by the future Major-General J. F. C. Fuller, who served as the Tank Corp's Chief of Staff, in his *Plan 1919*. Fuller's plan involved three distinct phases and relied upon mechanised forces closely supported by air power. The first phase was to be carried out by a Disorganising Force which would strike deep into the enemy's hinterland, destroying his headquarters and paralysing his command apparatus. The second would involve a breaking or holding action elsewhere along the front intended to tie down the bulk of the enemy forces which, left leaderless and confused, would ultimately collapse. The third phase would involve a pursuit of up to 150 miles. Whether Fuller's plan could have been executed by the creaky tanks of the period is a matter for conjecture, but they followed the path of evolution to the point at which, two decades later, they could and did perform the roles he envisaged. *Plan 1919* is the foundation stone upon which the Blitzkrieg technique has been built, although the lessons of the Second World War and the Arab-Israeli wars tend to confirm that the best results are obtained if Phase II, the breaking or holding phase, runs concurrently with or, better still, actually precedes the deep penetration Phase I; again, experience shows that the destruction induced by Phases I and II is often so complete that the Phase III pursuit is superfluous.

As General Sir John Hackett has commented, the term Blitzkrieg is not altogether an accurate means of describing operations of this type, although it has now entered common usage and is clearly here to stay. Such operations, as the word 'Lightning' implies, were indeed conducted with speed, immense violence and initial surprise, but they succeeded because of *sustained* action and *unremitting pressure* throughout. The term first came into use as a means of describing the nature of the runaway series of victories won by the German Army and the Luftwaffe between 1939 and 1941, although this fails to take into account three very important factors. The first is the traditional German approach to war known as the Annihilation Concept (*Vernichtungsgedanke*), the object of which is to encircle the enemy in a large-scale recreation of the Battle of Cannae and destroy him where he stands. Fuller's plan shifted the emphasis from the enemy's flank to his rear, but the ideas dovetailed providing the means were available. General Manstein was the first to recognise that they were and the result was Germany's complete victory in the west in May-June 1940. The second factor was the German conduct of war at the operative or corps level. At this period most armies thought only in terms of strategy and tactics, respectively the planning of campaigns and the manner in which they are fought. The Germans, however, placed great emphasis on the intermediate operative level, forming their panzer divisions into panzer corps which themselves formed part of panzer groups and, later, panzer armies; the benefits accruing from such concentrations of force, capable of responding quickly to demands conveyed by an efficient command, control and communications structure, need no further emphasis. The third factor was that the German Army of the Second World War really consisted of one army within another. The panzer, motorised and *panzergrenadier* formations possessed complete mobility and acted as the spearhead for the rest. The non-mechanised formations, which constituted approximately 80 per cent of the Army's total strength, relied almost exclusively on the horse as a prime mover for their artillery and transport and their mobility was therefore only comparable to that of their 18th and 19th century forebears. The lesson of this is expressed concisely by General Dr F. M. von Senger und Etterlin, a former Commander-in-Chief Allied Forces Central Europe: 'Where one element within an army possesses a degree of mobility much superior to the rest, it should not be dispersed by being scattered around at the lower tactical level but concentrated into independent formations at the exclusive disposal of the highest possible command level.' For the first years of the Second World War the *Panzerwaffe* was controlled by professionals, but after Hitler assumed the mantle of the Army's Commander-in-Chief it was Germany's misfortune that this priceless asset was squandered in one ill-conceived venture after another.

Following the development of shaped-charge ammunition capable of penetrating the thickest armour, the second half of the war also witnessed the end of the tank's undisputed reign as 'Queen of the Battlefield', the outcome of operations turning more and more upon a tight tactical interlock between tanks, infantry, artillery and air support to suppress local opposition. As well, by 1944 commanders were accustomed to the mechanics of the Blitzkrieg technique and less likely to be thrown off balance by its application. For example, the principal thrust line of the German Ardennes offensive that December was soon identified and quickly blocked by using mobility to counter mobility, the result being the notorious but short-lived 'Bulge'.

The Second World War also witnessed advances in aeronautical technology which introduced a third dimension to the land battle. This was not simply evolutionary progress in the field of ground support and interdiction, which had been introduced during the First World War, but rather the ability to deliver an attack deep within the enemy's rear by means of parachute or air-landing troops. Yet however attractive this means of securing a strategic objective by *coup de main* may have seemed, the truth was that there were as many failures to record as there were successes. The Soviet Army had pioneered the techniques of the large-scale parachute drop in the 1930s but its airborne operations against the Wehrmacht usually ended in complete disaster, although it was able to report some successes in Manchuria as the war drew to its close. The Germans enjoyed some early successes in Scandinavia and the Low Countries, but the cost of the *Fallschirmjäger*'s greatest victory, the airborne invasion of Crete, was so prohibitively high that Hitler forbade further operations of this kind. British and American airborne operations in Normandy and north west Europe produced a higher incidence of success than failure, the most notable of the latter being at Arnhem, yet statistically the risks incurred remained too high for peace of mind.

There can be no gainsaying the fact that many airborne operations were brilliantly conceived, planned and executed. Equally, there is no disputing that the airborne assault was subject to so many variable influences that luck, good or bad, could affect its result. The troops themselves were at high risk during their descent and, once on the ground, had to rally into their tactical sub-units before the first objectives could be stormed. They were lightly equipped and vulnerable to counter-attack by an enemy who possessed AFVs,

Below: **The conventional view of the Soviet offensive: tanks and APCs approach the objective closely supported by fixed-wing jet aircraft. (***Novosti***)**

Above: **A flight of Yak-24 Horse twin-rotor transport helicopters leaves the ground.** (*Novosti*)

artillery and heavy weapons. By their very nature, the airborne operations of the Second World War were of short duration, the paratroopers being required to hold the captured objective while a relief force fought its way through to them in the shortest time possible.

In the 40 years which have elapsed since the Second World War military technology has continued to advance at an ever-increasing pace. Every army worthy of the name is now fully mechanised and equipped with sophisticated tanks, self-propelled artillery, armoured personnel carriers and assault engineer vehicles. The NBC factor has simply accelerated the inevitable necessity of getting troops onto tracks and behind armour on a potential battlefield where the quantum of firepower available defeats the imagination of the Second World War veteran. New types of armour have been introduced, giant strides have been made in gun and ammunition design and computerised fire control systems have been installed in main battle tanks. The means of target acquisition and destruction, both on the ground and in the air, have reached terrifying peaks of efficiency. The range at which the tank battle can be

fought has opened to the point where the limiting factor, on a European battlefield at least, has become interdictions on the line of sight imposed by the landscape itself, while the accelerated pace at which operations are conducted is accepted as a minimum requirement. Yet there is nothing really radical in any of this, for the various families of fighting vehicles and fixed-wing combat aircraft, together with their respective weapon systems, are simply products of the evolutionary process; in short, they perform the same functions as the Second World War AFVs and aircraft from which they are descended, but they perform them with the in-built advantage of two generations of technological progress. It is true that the massed use of Sagger ATGWs by the Egyptian Army during the opening phases of the 1973 Arab-Israeli War caused such a flutter that several instant-opinion television commentators promptly predicted the demise of the AFV. This took little account of the fact that the tactical situation was unique in itself and unlikely to be repeated elsewhere. Moreover, within days the Israelis had overcome this difficulty by adding mechanised infantry and artillery to their tank-heavy armoured divisions, the volume of fire produced making the Sagger operator's task almost impossible. In the final analysis, the Sagger problem was simply an evolution of that posed by the *Panzerfaust* in 1943, which was similarly countered by interlocking infantry/tank tactics.

In the field of airborne warfare the impact of technical change is less apparent. Every first class army possesses a highly respected airborne element; the Soviet Army maintains no less than eight airborne divisions, one of which is permanently committed to the fighting in Afghanistan. Today's paratrooper enjoys the benefit of excellent troop-carrying aircraft equipped with efficient navigating devices, improved parachute designs which permit lower drops, and greatly enhanced firepower. The majority of parachute drops made since 1945 have been entirely successful, although they were smaller in scope than those of the Second World War. Nevertheless, the high risk factors remain and it is difficult to conceive large scale drops being carried out in a Third World War scenario without crippling losses in men and machines, not least during the fly-in phase.

However, one does not need a crystal ball to see that it is in this third dimension that the future development of the land battle lies. With the exception of mass-destruction nuclear weapons which, if they serve their purpose correctly, will never be used, the only weapon system to be developed since 1945 which is capable of radically affecting the conduct of land warfare is that based on the helicopter. Helicopters first saw extensive military use in Korea and French Indo-China, generally in the reconnaissance and casualty evacuation roles. After the turboshaft engine was introduced in 1955, which provided a satisfactory power-to-weight ratio, and the simultaneous solving of several more technical problems associated with helicopter construction, the number entering service rose dramatically as designers produced rotorcraft for every conceivable military requirement, including troop transports, ground attack gunships, tank hunters, cargo carriers and flying cranes. From this moment, the influence of the helicopter on the land battle was never in doubt, because it offered the precision and flexibility which were previously lacking in airborne operations, and yet it possessed a degree of firepower equal to that of many AFVs.

The first major use of this new airmobility was seen in Vietnam, where the fluid tactical situation demanded a rapid response which only the helicopter could provide. The US Army's 1st Cavalry Division (Airmobile), conceived with airmobility as its principal asset, possessed no less than 428 rotorcraft. It arrived in Vietnam in August 1965 with a strength of 16,000 men, and was in action almost continuously, inflicting hitherto unheard-of casualties on its elusive communist opponents. During the much misunderstood Tet offensive of 1968 the firepower of the AH-1 Cobra proved to be a major factor in what amounted to the virtual destruction of the Vietcong.

Today, the 101st Air Assault Division, descended directly (and significantly) from the crack 101st Airborne Division, forms a major element of the United States' rapid reaction forces and is maintained permanently at a high state of alert. The division possesses three air assault brigades each of three battalions, an artillery regiment with two 105 mm M-198 howitzer battalions and one 155 mm M-198 howitzer battalion, plus air defence, engineer and signal units. In addition to enjoying the support of its attack helicopters, its ground troops can deploy 198 TOW ATGW launchers and 366 Dragon anti-tank missile systems. Flying at a height not exceeding 200 ft (60 m) above the nap of the earth, the division can arrive at its strategic objective ready-formed into its tactical sub-units, fly in its heavy weapons quickly, consolidate its position, defeat local counterattacks and even engage in local offensive operations while re-supply and casualty evacuation take place on its landing zones. Its capacity for protracted operations exceeds that of the airborne division by a wide margin.

The Soviet Army has followed suit more slowly but in recent years has devoted a steadily increasing proportion of its resources to helicopter formations. It is possible that their thinking has its roots in the 1973 Arab-Israeli War. In its weight and scope the Syrian attack on the Golan was the closest thing we are likely to see to an armour-led offensive against NATO's Central Front, and it had the benefit of three factors which the Soviets deem essential: strategic surprise, overwhelming strength at the point of assault, and high motivation amongst its participants. However, the offensive failed, and the reasons for its failure included equal motivation and better tank gunnery from the outnumbered Israelis, who held on just long enough for their reserve armoured formations to mobilise and reach the front. One of the lessons from this war was that equipment of all kinds is now subject to a rate of destruction which is without parallel in military history, and as the means of defeating armour have been extensivly improved since 1973, it is inevitable that this rate has accelerated.

It seems, therefore, that in the two-dimensional battle the balance between attack and defence is again inclining towards the latter. For the Soviets the implications in this are extremely serious, for all the evidence suggests that if they ever did mount an offensive against NATO they would seek a quick kill in the Blitzkrieg tradition; there are, in fact, inherent flaws in the Soviet Army and the Soviet system generally which render anything less than a rapid, outright victory an unjustifiable risk. The Syrian reverse on the Golan was thus a matter for the most serious concern, not only because of the bad publicity it generated, but also because checks of such magnitude could seriously jeopardise the entire concept of success on a Central European battlefield.

Against this, Soviet doctrine emphasises that a battle must be fought throughout the entire depth of an enemy's position, and in practical terms this means maximum use of third dimensional assets. In 1979 the Soviets began forming airborne assault brigades which, although they wear the uniform of the airborne forces, are airmobile in concept. Each airborne assault brigade consists of three airborne battalions, one helicopter assault regiment, one squadron of heavy assault helicopters, and technical support units. Originally available only to front commanders, their numbers have now increased to the point where they are being incorporated into the order of battle of tank armies, and they are clearly intended for use at the operative level. These troops are specialists and should not be confused with the one motor rifle battalion in three which receives some airmobile training during its annual cycle. They can be reinforced with the air-portable BMD IFV and the ASU-85 assault gun, both of which can be air-

landed within a secure DZ or para-dropped on a pallet. The Soviets gained valuable experience in this area during the 1978 Ogaden War between Ethiopia and Somalia, in which they were responsible for a number of parachute and airmobile operations which defeated the Somalis and which involved the use of 70 of the older air-portable ASU-57 assault guns. Although the conflict was treated as a comparatively minor event in the West, the Soviet Union took it so seriously that General Vasili Petrov, then First Deputy Commander of Ground Forces, was detailed to plan and co-ordinate the Ethiopian counter-offensive.

In his book *Red Armour* Richard Simpkin extends the

The Mi-10 Harke heavy-lift/flying crane helicopter in Aeroflot livery. (*Novosti*)

view expressed by the defector 'Viktor Suvorov' that the Soviets now regard the helicopter as a lightly armoured tank which is not inhibited by such features as water obstacles, woodland, built-up areas and minefields. In Soviet eyes the same mobility differential now exists between rotorcraft and mechanised formations as existed in the Second World War between the latter and marching infantry divisions with horse-drawn impedimenta. Moreover, the Soviets have recognised the potential of that part of their army which so clearly possesses a superior mobility and have concentrated it in formations at the disposal of senior commanders. Whether they will, as General von Senger suggests regarding superior mobility assets in general, expand their airborne assault brigades into divisions or corps at the *exclusive disposal of the highest possible command level*, remains a matter for conjecture.

This latest turn in the evolutionary spiral will naturally result in a marked increase in the tempo at which operations are conducted. In the Second World War the German panzer formations, having secured a breakthrough, motored on to distant objectives, covered all the time by the Luftwaffe. In their wake came the hard-marching infantry, lining the shoulders of the penetration and eliminating pockets of resistance which had been created by the tank spearheads. Over 40 years

Above: A flight of Mi-24 Hind helicopter gunships practice nap-of-the-earth flying during Exercise Nemen. (*Novosti*)

Left: The Mi-24 Hind also serves as an armed assault transport. Note the array of ground-attack weapons mounted on the stub-wings.

Previous page: **Mi-8 Hip assault transport helicopters and a battery of air-portable ASU-85 assault guns illustrate one aspect of Soviet airmobile potential.** (*Novosti*)

on, helicopter formations do not need to secure a break-through and, given the lion's share of the available air cover, can reach distant objectives in fraction of the time previously required. In this context, armoured and mechanised formations will perform the same roles once carried out by the infantry, but at a vastly increased pace. The effect is comparable to the addition of overdrive to a standard gearbox.

Fuller's genius lay in harnessing the technical resources which were available and using them to solve the battlefield problems of his time. If he were to write his *Plan 1919* today he would probably not alter its structure but, great innovator that he was, he would undoubtedly decide that his Phase I must be executed by helicopter formations. The essence of his thinking lay in striking the fatal blow in the right place at the right time and, as the American Civil War general might have put it, that involves 'getting there firstest with the mostest.'

FIBUA and the Weapons System Concept

S. S. Fitz-Gibbon

It is an accepted fact that any major European conflict in the foreseeable future will include a considerable level of fighting in built-up areas. What is somewhat less predictable is which side is most likely to be successful. Warsaw Pact organisation and tactics tend to be quite different from those of NATO, and within the Atlantic Alliance there are several different philosophies on how to fight the urban battle. Indeed, within each national army there are probably several shades of opinion, if not widely differing schools of thought, on this one subject of great importance. Wartime experience abounds, but such experience varies widely between different armies, and even in the same army between one battle and another. This is perhaps because an infinite number of variables, often outside the control of the forces concerned, influence the course of an engagement, and conclusions may be drawn from the same action that vary considerably between analysts viewing the question from different angles. What I believe is necessary to illuminate this most shady of subjects is a formula which is based on the relative certainties of the problem, which permits the flexibility necessary to provide for all eventualities, and which can therefore be adapted to cover the vagaries as they occur. While it is not suggested that there is ever a 'final solution' to any continually developing military problem, it is probable that such a formula can be found which will allow organisation and methods to develop according to requirements, and which will permit the flexibility necessary for adapting to rapidly changing and sometimes unforeseeable events as they occur on the ground.

The medium through which I wish to view the subject is therefore that of the concept of the weapons system. This concept is covered in greater detail elsewhere, but its main point is this: that every military unit or formation, from the front or army group to the fire team or patrol, should be considered a complete entity in its own right – a 'weapons system' in which thoughts and ideas have led, along parallel lines, to weapons technology and battle drills, instituting an organisational structure and a set of functions based on perception of the system's tactical objectives, its capabilities and its need to survive confrontation with hostile systems. Any analysis of an engagement, whether past or predicted, must take into account these factors. Those who do not appreciate that the interlocking of the system's elements is the key factor – who attribute a force's success in battle to one factor, such as its commander or a particular regiment or weapon or tactic – therefore see only a part of the picture. For example FIBUA (Fighting in Built-Up Areas) has often been described as an 'infantry battle', but the submission here is that this is a blinkered view. Even to say that the infantry fight the urban battle with the support of the other arms is to underestimate the importance of those other arms, since it can easily give the impression that the infantry could have done the job on their own, albeit with a little greater difficulty. The only acceptable view, in my opinion, is to treat the FIBUA force as a *system* in which each component – infantry, tanks, combat engineers, artillery and so on – is a vital element without which the system is out of balance and can only be successful if it is disproportionately numerically superior or prepared to accept a crippling casualty rate, or both. Perhaps the best rebuttal of the 'infantry battle' theory is provided by the protracted period of signally inconclusive fighting by largely unsupported infantry in Beirut in recent years.

An apt illustration of the 'weapons system' concept is found in the development of FIBUA techniques by the Soviets during the Second World War. According to the

(a)

(b)

Above:
a. FIBUA drills are now as important to soldiers as any, and must be practised by both day and night.
b. It is usually preferable to enter a building by an upper window, but without ladders this can be slow and tiring.
c. FIBUA requires special drills, but basic principles of fire covering movement remain unaltered. (*S.S. Fitz-Gibbon***)**

Below: **Entry techniques and rapid clearance drills must be second nature. Equipment should be stripped to the minimum – not forgetting that large quantities of grenades and small arms ammunition must be carried, along with adequate supplies of water and field dressings. NBC suits are cumbersome, but help prevent burns. (***S.S. Fitz-Gibbon***)**

above definitions the Red Army weapons system was quite unbalanced for much of the war, but was at its most coherent and deadly during some of the later urban battles. The tactics and organisation employed departed to a large extent from general Soviet practices and witnessed an uncharacteristic flexibility and cohesion between arms – evidence firstly of the creative thought which is the life-blood of a weapons system and secondly of the interaction of functions which is its central nervous system. The standard combat unit for FIBUA purposes was known as the 'storm detachment', which possessed an infantry battalion, a company of tanks, two batteries of artillery (one tracked and one towed), an engineer company with demolition and

isolated in preparation for the assault, which would be made in a series of concentric blows inwards, dividing the defenders into small pockets. Of course, the aim was for the first troops to by-pass the enemy if possible, leaving the task of their destruction in detail to the succeeding echelon. After an unusually detailed reconnaissance, a devastating fire-strike would hit the objective for about 40 minutes, and then the infantry would immediately begin a rapid advance with close support. When opposition was encountered, the fire support groups would close up and hammer the objective. Artillery was often fired at point-blank range and Katyusha rocket launchers backed around corners to flatten entire rows of houses. Heavy machine guns and light anti-tank guns could be manhandled over rubble and through buildings to give support where tanks and heavier guns could not move. The storm group itself would break down into a fire group, an assault group and a consolidation group, and would assault with the invaluable assistance of armour and combat engineers. Well-practised clearance drills were carried out before the consolidation group closed in. A rapid reorganisation was carried out in order to prevent a successful counter-attack, and the momentum of the assault was continued. Even with this amount of non-infantry firepower, concentration of force was of paramount importance; the storm detachment described above might have had as its initial objective just one block of buildings.

It is a fitting testimony to the success of this flexible and streamlined system that when it was changed and became unbalanced, its success was severely reduced. When the proven method of intimate mutual support

smoke-laying equipment, a flamethrower platoon, and probably additional supporting sub-units. The storm detachment usually divided into a 'fire support group' based on an infantry company and nominally controlled by the battalion commander, and between two and six 'storm groups' each with an infantry strength of one or two platoons or a company, intimately supported by tanks, engineers and other assets. This order of battle retained a flexibility to reorganise itself according to circumstances without having to place sub-units under command of other regiments from which we today could do well to learn.

The Soviets' tactics were simple but crushingly effective. The objective would be surrounded and

Above: **A tank commander's view of the British 'Crocodile' flamethrower tank in use in 1944.**

with infantry as the major and leading component was departed from during the Soviet assault on Berlin, the result was quite disastrous. Leading with tanks only loosely supported by infantry, the Soviets sustained 200,000 casualties in a week, and some 64 per cent of the armour of 2nd Guards Tank Army was destroyed. The fact that much of this destruction was caused by infantry anti-tank weapons goes a long way to proving the value of treating an armed force as a single system of integral and interlocking parts.[1]

In view of the fact that the Soviets base their system today on the all-arms divisions of the war, developed to suit changing circumstances – for example, with enhanced artillery support and with increasing emphasis on FIBUA in their training – it may be pertinent to ask the question 'Does the British Army compare favourably with its potential adversary?' In answering this question, one major criticism springs to mind. In the British Army the principal administrative organisations, the regiments and battalions, are not the same as the primary combat grouping, the battle groups. An infantry-heavy battle group, the kind most likely to be involved in FIBUA, has a battalion of infantry or less, plus a squadron of tanks, a battery of artillery and the necessary reconnaissance, engineer, signal, air-defence and anti-tank guided weapon assets attached from other regiments. This can be fairly regarded as putting the British Army at a disadvantage compared to the Soviets and others for two reasons: firstly, since the groupings are temporary, the various sub-units do not train together as frequently as they should and are consequently often quite ignorant of each other's methods and value in battle, as well as lacking the coherence which comes from continual co-operation on training exercises. Secondly, the officer's and soldier's first loyalty is to his regiment, or sometimes to his battalion, with group cohesion strongest at company or platoon level in most cases. The dominant attitude tends to be one of contemptuous competition rather than comradely co-operation, and the resulting rivalry is often less than friendly and frequently results in the damaging factionalism which has led, on occasions, to serious failings in battle.[2] This already far-from-ideal situation is worsened by the Army's commissioning system, which tends to produce an officer of the 'regimental' persuasion with little knowledge and probably no real experience of other arms. Such 'other arms' training is given only in an introductory form at RMAS and the arms schools, and all-arms warfare training and cross-posting opportunities are quite inadequate. While these are points of concern for the Army as a whole, they are decisively more pressing in the case of a battle group finding itself on the brink of an urban battle. History shows that mutual support in built-up areas must not be merely close, but intimate; combined arms battle drills must be second nature, and *esprit de corps* must be at a very high level. In these matters the British battle group system seems to fall down quite badly.

Fortunately, however, all is not so unpromising. FIBUA training in the British Army is increasing and improving, and it is taken very seriously indeed by both officers and soldiers. Excellent FIBUA training centres exist at Longmoor and Whinny Hill, and Imber Village gives troops operating on Salisbury Plain a small built-up area in which to operate. The Bundeswehr's superb FIBUA complex at Hammelberg in Bavaria, a village of some size, is available to British troops, and the excellent Ruhleben 'fighting city' provides the Berlin brigade with an urban training ground. Recently, a decision was taken to build more such complexes, so training opportunities look set to improve even more.

Furthermore, the Army is beginning to recognise certain of its weaknesses in this sphere. An important exercise known as 'King's Ride' was recently held in Germany with a view to testing both British and Soviet-type tactics in attack and defence, in order to highlight any failings. One of its many conclusions was that certain assistional weapons would greatly enhance our

---

Below: **Infantry assault, closely supported by armour, on Exercise King's Ride V. (Note SAWES – Small Arms Weapons Effects Simulator – attachments on personnel and weapons).** (*J.M. Lynam*)

capability, and this has been confirmed by other sources. A study by the School of Infantry found that the flamethrower, a weapon regarded as indispensable in the urban battles of the Second World War and one relied upon to a great extent by the Soviets today, is a weapon urgently needed for FIBUA. Suggestions by the officers of a Territorial Army battalion tasked with the defence of a largely urbanised area in West Germany in 1 British Corps' general deployment plan, that some method of projecting grenades over greater distances and with more accuracy would be most useful, were supported by the troops involved in Exercise King's Ride. Whether these suggestions are acted upon, however, remains to be seen.[3]

It is with the above experiences and the 'weapons system' doctrine in mind that I wish to suggest tentatively a series of improvements in structure and function which, I believe, could produce an urban warfare force appropriately organised, equipped and trained to respond effectively to any conventional urban threat.

The first conclusion drawn must point inevitably to closer adherence to the weapons system concept. This would entail raising the status of the infantry battalion to that of an all-arms battle group, permanently established and with all its supporting sub-units wearing the same cap-badge as its infantry companies. Moreover, the doctrine of mutual support should be carried down to company and platoon levels. Since mutual support between companies in the restricting environment of a built-up area is difficult if not impossible to achieve, and since companies will often find themselves operating independently of, or unintentionally isolated from, battalion HQ, it may be advisable to have some of the support arms in the company order of battle, with the ability to concentrate these at battalion level if necessary. Because platoon defended posts will find themselves isolated from neighbouring platoons, the platoon must be better able to look after itself, and so must possess an enhanced fire support capability. Again, since sections may find themselves cut off, either in attack or in defence, or may be used frequently as local quick-reaction forces for counter-penetration fighting patrols or for ambushes during a defence or withdrawal phase, the section should accordingly be up-gunned. Increasing the size of the platoon and the section could also help to offset the heavier casualty rate likely in FIBUA.

The order of battle suggested would include four infantry companies, permitting considerable flexibility. The companies would be larger than at present, partly because of the additional support weapons on their establishment and partly because their three rifle platoons would be increased by about one-third to 40 all ranks. This would allow each ten-man section to possess two identical fire teams equipped as planned with the SA80 series small arms, and also a two-man fire support

group with a General Purpose Machine gun (GPMG) and an additional Light Support Weapon (LSW). To the normal HQ element of commander, second-in-command, signaller and runner would be added a GPMG support group of three men, and the light mortar element would be increased from one man to three, firstly so that much more ammunition could be carried and secondly to provide two additional platoon runners if required as an alternative, and often more reliable, means of communication.

The extra weapons required would be varied to give commanders a greater range of alternatives in use. A company of tanks would be essential, especially in the attack or counter-attack. The artillery would be self-propelled so that it could be used in the close support direct fire role. Engineer resources would be substantial, including considerable stocks of demolition stores, Bangalore torpedoes, smoke generators and mines. Off-route mines are better suited than buried anti-tank mines to an urban environment, especially with the introduction by the Soviets of ERA (Explosive Reactive Armour) on the T-80 and T-64B tanks, greatly increasing their protection on the side and frontal arcs. Firing off-route mines down from buildings into their turret tops or engine compartments might be one of the best ways of dealing with them. Claymore-type mines are invaluable for defence, withdrawal and ambush, and Ranger rapidly-laid anti-personnel mines would be most useful for covering withdrawals or trapping enemy infantry in the killing grounds. As well as the standard vehicle-mounted Ranger dispenser, a man-portable four-tube launcher is now available. Milan and Swingfire assets will be confined by their present task of perimeter defence, their use within built-up areas being restricted by the length of time between the launch of the missile and its coming under control of the operator, and moreover being limited by their inability to cause sufficient damage to buildings if used in support of an assault. Strongly armoured reconnaissance troops would be essential for destroying enemy reconnaissance elements and thereby preventing detailed survey of friendly positions. As well as the battalion armoured reconnaissance platoon, I would suggest a two-vehicle recce section at company level. This would have important tasks in fire support, flank protection and counter-attack. If the infantry are carried in non-armoured vehicles their cannon and machine guns

would be all the more vital. And if vehicles such as the Dragoon multi-mission vehicle were chosen, they could double as MICVs for a quick reaction force. I would also suggest the formation of a sniper section at battalion level, with five pairs for distribution as required.

Additional weaponry not currently held by the British Army needs to be acquired, and some older weapons retained or brought back into service. The Wombat 120 mm recoilless anti-tank gun has been replaced in its intended role, but it would most definitely fill a gap in the infantry armoury. When tanks and assault guns are not available, or cannot move over rubble or into narrow gaps, only the Wombat could be as effective in holing a wall or destroying a building. Two guns per company are suggested, each with a section of ten men so that they rely neither on towing vehicles nor on the infantry sections to move them into their firing positions, along with their heavy and bulky ammunition. The GPMG, which is being largely replaced by the LSW, is most useful for its ability to cut through brick walls, hence its suggested retention in every rifle section. Flamethrowers are absolutely necessary, on a scale of about two per company. Rifle grenades would greatly benefit riflemen, especially in the assault. Modern types are available which require no

Top: **Infantry anti-tank weapons are essential for small-scale operations, such as ambushes, likely in FIBUA.** (*J.M. Lynam*)

Above: **Off-route mine trainer in use. Off-route mines bolster up anti-armour ambushes.** (*J.M. Lynam*)

additional attachment to the weapon or a special cartridge to fire them, but are simply fitted on to the rifle muzzle and projected by firing whatever round happens to be in the chamber into a bullet trap in the grenade tail.

An additional small-arm which is suggested for issue to each platoon is some form of shotgun. Its principal use would be to break down doors and window frames prior to entry during the assault, in order to activate any booby-traps. Although external doors and windows are not ideal entry points, they are sometimes the only ones available and entry to the inner rooms through doors is inevitable. The use of shotguns in such circumstances would also help to economise on grenades.

In order to improve the indirect fire support capability of the FIBUA system, the battalion should have 16 mortars rather than the usual eight. Half of these would be distributed to the rifle companies. While the battalion mortars would be used against enemy approaching the battalion strongpoint, or in the initial bombardment prior to an assault, it is felt that the special characteristics of FIBUA render the medium mortar a useful company support weapon. The main difficulty with using any indirect fire weapon in towns is the probable inability of the fire controller to see the precise location of the fall of shot and to direct the fire onto targets by radio communication with the mortars. Where the mortar baseplate is a long way from the controller, the difficulty increases, since VHF communications are hampered by screening. But mortars can still be used in two important ways without the necessity to direct the fire by sight. Firstly, defensive fire tasks can be registered before battle commences, so that on the appearance of an enemy the mortars can open fire on him at short notice. If VHF communication was impossible or difficult and land-lines had been cut by shelling, Defensive Fire (DF) tasks could be activated by simple light or visual signals by observers closer to the target. Secondly, mortars can be used to engage depth targets in the assault, moving just a tactical bound ahead of the assaulting troops and using their high trajectory to good effect. When an assault group reports that is has secured its objectives the mortars simply switch their fire to the next objective for a predetermined period before it is assaulted and so on. An additional way to improve communications for this and other purposes would be to increase the line-laying facilities within the battalion and company. The Soviet Army are known to be improving this aspect of their signals arm.

The final requirement for the FIBUA-oriented weapons system would be that the training of its personnel must be intensively modified. What I suggest is a battalion of FIBUA specialists. This would by no means preclude their use in other kinds of warfare; it is simply an acceptance of the fact that FIBUA has very special characteristics and requires exceptionally fit, well-trained and exercised, highly motivated troops. Royal Marines and paratroopers would be ideal, but they have other specialist tasks and much of their training would be wasted in a primarily 1 British Corps' FIBUA role. Guards and Gurkhas would fit the bill, but there is a danger of putting all our existing elite eggs in the same highly dangerous urban basket. The requirement would be for a small number of battalions organised as outlined above and welded into an elite body like the regiments already mentioned. The greater need for initiative in junior commanders in urban battles must be taken into account, and only recruits of above average intellect accepted. Their basic training must include a selection process on the lines of that for the Royal Marine Commando course or the Army's preparachute selection, in order to ensure the desired level of fitness and motivation. Such a selection test, perhaps rewarded by some honour comparable with the marine's green or paratrooper's red beret – which all members of the battalion, including the non-infantry companies would have to earn – would undoubtedly form the basis for an admirable system of elite combat motivation.

Summary

The special characteristics of warfare in urban areas require a different mode of thought from other operations. Factors which are important in other types of terrain become crucial in built-up areas, and battle conditions demand a more finely-tuned, streamlined weapons system. That the British Army is now giving more attention to FIBUA, not just in unit training but in tactical analysis and the consideration of additional types of equipment essential in street fighting, is a most welcome development. It is to be hoped that the current phase of active and critical thought should manifest itself in a call for improvements which is sufficiently loud to override the conservative noises which often cause creative suggestions in the Army to go unheard.

References

1. School of Infantry, Warminster; Video recording 'FIBUA Part II: The Soviet View'.
2. Anthony Kellet's article 'The Regimental System and Combat Motivation' in *Jane's Military Review*, 5th Ed 1986, gives an adequate and concise explanation of this factor.
3. Exercise King's Ride is described in *Army Training News*, spring 1986.

The Spanish Army Approaches its Future

X. I. Taibo

Not strictly in connection with recent integration into NATO, the Spanish Army is carrying out a considerable transformation of its structure under the META plan. Its guidelines are to obtain a smaller, more professional, better equipped and faster reacting organisation, able to defend the country in the face of today's menaces and technologies.

The Former Organisation

Prior to 1965, Franco's army had a heavy structure with an impressive number of divisions; large in manpower but with a strikingly poor equipment. In that year a new organisation was adopted, in which the main unit was the brigade, although a smaller number of divisions (five) was kept. Still too large, the Army had to select a number of privileged units to receive updated equipment and to be kept close to full manpower establishment, while a number of others were maintained well under minimum standards both in staff and equipment. A first discrimination was thus established; the 'Immediate Intervention' units and the 'Operational Defence of Territory' units.

The *Intervención Inmediata* units consisted of an Army corps with three infantry divisions (armoured, mechanised and motorised), plus support units such as a cavalry brigade, an artillery brigade and regiments/battalions of other corps. In addition the parachute and air transportable brigades were included. Every division had two brigades (combining three different infantry brigade types) plus support units of several specialities, with the scope for absorbing a third brigade in wartime. In fact, although this structure of ten brigades had almost all the armoured fighting vehicles in the Spanish Army, it was widely spread throughout the country and kept close to full manpower, although shortages in equipment were still apparent.

The *Defensa Operativa del Territorio* forces were connected with local operations and had no priority at all, either in manpower recruitment or in equipment, except for those units stationed in the Canaries and in Africa, and particularly the Spanish Legion. Two mountain divisions existed, but each had only one brigade plus support units, with added a second brigade to each division on mobilisation. The other brigades in the territorial defence structure were the High Mountain Brigade, the Reserve Infantry Brigade, nine light infantry brigades for the nine military regions, and a coastal and anti-aircraft artillery brigade for the Straits. The Balearic Islands had units similar in size to one territorial infantry brigade, and the Canaries similar to two brigades. Their low level can be illustrated by realising that every one of the nine regional brigades was to have six infantry battalions and two artillery groups in wartime, while their theoretical peacetime strength was only two infantry battalions – even those probably below their establishment –and one artillery group, plus cavalry and engineers. Until recently they had no armoured vehicles, though in the past few years they finally received a light tank company of 16 M-41 tanks per brigade.

The META Plan

Approved by the government in 1984, the META plan was destined to make considerable changes to obtain a

Above: **In continuous production, the 6 × 6 Pegaso BMR-600 armoured infantry fighting vehicle is being delivered to a number of infantry and cavalry units of the Spanish Army, in addition to successful export sales.**

smaller army with much more homogeneous units brought up to full establishment in peacetime. META stands for *Modernizacion del Ejercito de Tierra* (Modernisation of the Land Army) though the word 'meta', appropriately enough, also means 'goal' in Spanish. The main outlines of the plan are as follows:

    – a smaller number of units with higher equipment standards;

    – a more homogeneous structure for all the specialised types of formation;

    – existing units to be, in peacetime, close to wartime establishment in both manpower and equipment;

    – the brigade-level units to be located in bases as complete units;

    – the logistic support in bases and barracks to be

independent of the based units themselves, so that they had their hands free for their own tasks;

    – considerable changes in logistic support for regions, now being carried out, with regional commands to be superseded by new commands each covering two existing regions;

    – the former nine regions in the Peninsula to be reduced to six;

    – major units to be located each in a single region, and both they and the minor units to depend, in most cases, on regional headquarters in peacetime for administration;

    – the number of units independent of brigades and divisions to be greatly reduced from the former organisation and to be largely specialised supporting units;

    – the former distinction between 'Immediate Intervention' and 'Territorial Defence' units no longer obtains:

    – the Army corps level to be no longer considered now, though it might eventually be formed in the future.

A comparison between former and new organisation of the Spanish Army: general characteristics

	Former organisation (1965, with subsequent changes)	New organisation (META plan)
Large formations:		
Divisions	Five, joining eight brigades	Five, joining eleven brigades
Independent brigades	16	Four
Type of brigade-sized units	Heterogeneous, some without logistics units and the artillery formations only as a mere sum of regiments of this corps	Homogeneous: all have one artillery group, one engineer battalion and one logistics group. Only various types of infantry and cavalry brigades
Minor formations	Numerous at regiment, battalion and company level, independent of divisions and brigades	Small number of specialised regiment or battalion-sized units independent of the larger formations
Extra-Peninsular formations (Balearic and Canary Islands, towns of Ceuta and Melilla)	A number of units expanded in all these locations, each under the joint command	Apparently only minor changes from the 1965 organisation, mainly reinforcing the island garrisons
Military regions in the Spanish Peninsula	Nine	Six

The Resulting Structure

The general unit structure once the META plan has been completed, is expected to be as follows:

1) Operational commands: six in the Peninsula, coinciding with the six new military regions, plus two in the Islands, which in peacetime will join both the large units and the minor garrison units
2) General Reserve units
3) Specialised Task units (*Unidades de cometidos específicos*)
4) General support logistic units.

The towns of Ceuta and Melilla, in northern Africa, are included in the Second Military Region, and they each have a special command, with forces close to division level. These, plus the Canary and Balearic Islands, do not have proper divisions or brigades, but their particular commands join all the small units located there.

Let us now look at the units so organised.

Divisions and Brigades

The META plan keeps unaltered the number and names of the five divisions existing from the 1965 re-organisation plan. However, their structures have undergone significant changes, mainly in the mountain divisions.

When the plan is completed, the five divisions will have two brigades each, plus support units, except for 2 Division, which has three brigades. All the divisions have a single-figure number, from 1 to 5, which means that the Mountain Division formerly numbered 6 is now 5 Division, because the division's number now coincides with the number of the military region in which it is located. Brigades have a two-figure number, where the first digit indicates the divisional number, but the brigade will always be identified by a Roman numeral. Thus the three brigades in 2 Division are XXI, XXII and XXIII.

The support units (*núcleo de tropas divisionario*) in every division consist of one light armoured cavalry regiment (except for the mountain divisions), one field artillery regiment, one anti-aircraft artillery group (again, except for the mountain divisions), one 'mixed' engineer regiment (where 'mixed' means that it has one pioneer and one signals battalion), one logistic unit (*agrupación*) of regimental level, and a new-style NBC company.

The specialised titles of infantry divisions and brigades, as seen in the former 1965 organisation, are usually omitted now, avoiding mention of the mechanised or motorised character of the unit, but quoting as armoured (*acorazada*) the 1 Division and its XII Brigade. However, more accurate sources from the Spanish Ministry of Defence consider that both brigades of 3 Division (Valencia area) can be said to be

mechanised, as much as XXI Brigade in 2 Division, whose two other brigades are motorised. 1 Division *Acorazada* has one mechanised (XI) and one armoured brigade (XII).

Thus the resulting locations of the three senior infantry divisions are as follows:

División Acorazada 'Brunete' No 1, with Brigades XI, recently moved from Madrid to Badajoz, and XII Armoured, near Madrid;

División 'Guzmán el Bueno' No 2, which is the only division with three brigades: XXI in the Córdoba area, XXII to be concentrated in the Campo de Gibraltar (Cádiz), and XXIII in the Almeria province. This last brigade originated directly from the former Infantry Reserve Brigade;

División 'Maestrazgo' No 3, with XXXI (Valencia) and XXXII (Cartagena) brigades.

The main arrangement of the brigades remains basically unaltered from their former organisation apart from the addition of an anti-tank company per brigade. Thus, apart from this company, they have one HQ company; four battalions of infantry of which one has tanks and some or all of the others are carried under armour, either in M113 APCs or on wheeled BMR-600 transporters; one artillery group (battalion) with 18 howitzers of either 155 mm or 105 mm calibre, self-propelled or towed; one 'mixed' engineer battalion; and a logistic group. The exception is the XII Armoured Brigade which has only three infantry battalions, two with tanks and the third in APCs.

The estimated strength of the normal division is in the region of 15,000, except for 2 Division which is close to 20,000.

The mountain divisions are, naturally, deployed in the Pyrenees. The META plan is to double the number of their brigades, but in any case they will be smaller and obviously much lighter than the three infantry divisions. The mountain units are:

División de Montaña 'Urgel' No 4, in Lleida (Lérida), with XLI Brigade in that town and XLII which is being formed from the distant origin of the old infantry Territorial Brigade No 4; and

División de Montaña 'Navarra' No 5 (previously No 6), headquarters in Burgos with Brigades LI (formerly LXI) in Donostia (San Sebastián) and LII, formed from the *Brigade de Alta Montaña* of Huesca.

The expected composition for the future mountain brigade is of three battalions of *cazadores* (light infantry) (four in wartime), one light 105 mm artillery group which can be mule-transported, one mountain engineer battalion and one logistic group.

Above left: **The Fiero 20 mm twin light anti-aircraft gun.**

Above: **The 105/26 light howitzer is of Spanish design, dating from 1950, and utilises the standard American M1 family of ammunition.**

The Independent Brigades

The number of brigades not included in divisions was 16 in the former organisation, but this has been reduced to four in the present and future one, mainly due to the progressive dismantling of the regional infantry brigades which were, as we have said, well under their organisational requirements. These four independent brigades are as follows:

Brigada Paracaidista in Alcalá de Henares, near Madrid;
Brigada Aerotransportable in the province of La Coruña (Corunna);
Brigadas de Caballeria Jarama (Salamanca and Old Castile) and *Castillejos* (Zaragoza).

The composition of the first two brigades is probably destined to be similar, but with different training due to

the dominance of parachute operations in the former, while the Air-Transportable Brigade is a light infantry brigade which can operate as a reserve brigade, either land- or air-mobile; both have, or will have, one HQ company, three rifle battalions (*banderas* in the Parachute Brigade) with the third battalion in the Air-Transportable Brigade to be formed from some disbanding regional brigade; one light artillery group of 18 105 mm howitzers; the usual engineer and logistic battalion-sized units and the addition of an anti-tank company, already formed in the Parachute Brigade. The attachment to brigades of their new anti-tank companies will be enhanced by the immediate disbandment of the 35 *Toledo* Anti-tank Regiment, which in the former organisation was kept in the Army corps support structure.

In the former organisation only one cavalry brigade existed also at Army corps level, the *Jarama* which was actually a super-brigade with four cavalry regiments and two artillery groups, some 6000 men and about 170 M-47 tanks. Very recently it was decided to form a second cavalry brigade to operate in the Aragon plains, and with its HQ in Zaragoza. Its strength originates from two cavalry regiments which were previously allocated to both mountain divisions. These have now lost their cavalry but can be supported by this brigade

placed in their rearguard, not far from the Pyrenees and in one of the military regions where they can be fitted. The new brigade *Castillejos* has also gained a third cavalry regiment from the oversized *Jarama* brigade, and we can assume that one of the two artillery groups of this will pass to the new brigade, thus leaving every brigade with three cavalry regiments, one artillery group (SP 105 mm with 18 howitzers) and the usual engineer battalion and logistics group.

Independent Units in the Peninsula

Beside these major units, a number of regimental or battalion-sized units fulfill the army's structure on the Peninsula. We can arrange them in an approximate way as follows:

Garrison units in the Peninsula: the former special operations companies are progressively being joined in *grupos*, each of three companies plus one service company. One *grupo* is being formed in each of the six reorganised regions, plus one in the Legion's 4 *Tercio*. Another infantry garrison unit is the *Agrupación de Tropas del Cuartel General*, in Madrid, and the Royal Guard, a regiment/brigade unit joining Army, Navy and Air Force troops under the Spanish name of *Guardia Real*.

As garrison units we must also consider the anti-aircraft and coastal artillery regiments. The four existing static anti-aircraft regiments (Nos 71 to 74) do not now belong to a common command, but are tied to the Air Force's defence net and there is a possibility that they may be integrated into the *Ejército del Aire* since most of them are destined for airfield defence. However the coastal artillery in the Peninsula has seen sharp regimental reductions in past years, and only four regiments remain, two of them in the Straits, where they formed part of the disbanded *Brigada de Artillería del Estrecho*. Since this kind of brigade without support units or services is no longer taken into consideration, these two regiments now form the *Mando de Artillería del Estrecho* (Artillery Command for the Straits), while an equipment programme for all coastal artillery in Spain is under consideration.

Thus the two regiments which formerly composed the *Brigada de Artillería para Cuerpo de Ejército* now belong to the new *Mando de Artillería del Ejército*; they

are the *Lanzacohetes* (rocket-launching) of Astorga and one heavy artillery regiment equipped with 203 mm howitzers. Probably included in this command are the field light anti-aircraft artillery regiment (formerly for Army corps) 26 of Valladolid and the *Regimiento de Información y Localización* (Information and Locating) in Ciudad Real.

Taking into account that in the Spanish Army both pioneers and signals belong to the same corps or *Arma de Ingenieros*, three regiments of it are now included in the *Reserva General*: the *Regimiento de Transmisiones* of El Pardo (near Madrid), being enriched with a new EW battalion for tactical purposes; the *Regimiento de Zapadores* (pioneers) located in Salamanca; and the *Regimiento de Pontoneros y Especialidades* (bridging and special tasks) in Zaragoza.

Unidades de Cometidos Específicos: these specialised task units are three engineer regiments with widespread branches, since they serve in all the territory. The *Regimiento de la Red Territorial de Mando y Servicios Especiales de Transmisiones* which takes care of the communications network and has recently expanded with an EW battalion for strategic duties; the *Regimiento de Movilización y Practicas de Ferrocarriles* and the *Regimiento de Zapadores Ferroviarios* engaged in railway operation.

Unidades de Apoyo Logístico General (General Logistic Support Units): in the regimental size, these are the following: *Agrupación de Intendencia* (supplies); *Agrupación de Sanidad, Regimiento de Automoviles, Agrupación de Tropas de Farmacia* and *Agrupación de Tropas de Veterinaria* are all stationed in Madrid.

At a regional level the former organisation included a number of logistic units of company or battalion size for supply, sanitary (medical), transport and other duties. The META plan has entirely disbanded and replaced them, firstly forming MALRE or *Mandos Logísticos Regionales*. However, soon after the experimental reorganisation in the 3 Military Region, which was the first to be carried out, it was decided that it ought to be more effective in handling inter-regional logistic requirements for each pair of new regions. Three MALRIZ or *Mandos Logísticos Interregionales* have thus been established in Seville, Madrid and Zaragoza. They include *agrupaciones* (regimental-level units) for sanitary (medical) assistance, supply and maintenance.

The Military Police also has a regional structure with company or platoon (*sección*) units, with about six companies to be established within each military region.

Left: **The 122 mm L/46 field gun is derived from the Soviet M.1931/37 (A-19) and has been refurbished over the last few years. The Spanish Army still has some 120 of these field guns, but their replacement is foreseen. Known as Model 390/2, this gun belongs to *Regimento* No 28 at Pontevedra.**

The Army Air Force

The FAMET or *Fuerzas Aeromóviles del Ejército de Tierra* has been expanding since its creation in the 1960s and, having only helicopters, today its inventory is bigger than the collective helicopter stock in all the other

Above: **The Santa Barbara SB 155/39 155 mm howitzer is currently undergoing evaluation trials for possible adoption by the Spanish Army.**

military and para-military services in Spain. The FAMET units are fully independent of major units and have a certain degree of specialisation:

A single attack helicopter battalion, the BHELA I with MBB 105 machines, is located at Almagro, Ciudad Real;

A single transport battalion, the BHELTRA V, near Madrid, flying Chinooks, might be followed by a second one after the current order for Super Puma machines begins deliveries;

Four general-purpose helicopter units – UHELs – in different locations such as Sevilla, Valencia, La Rioja and the Canary Islands;

The helicopter training units are located near Madrid.

The Spanish Legion and the Future Intervention Force

Originated early in this century in order to intervene in the colonial wars in Morocco, the Spanish Foreign

Legion has a particularly hard discipline and special training, being considered the elite unit in the Spanish Army, and its rather violent behaviour has caused frequent problems with civilian populations, despite the fact that today the Legion is no longer an all-volunteer force.

The Legion is organised at present in four *tercios*: the first three, *Gran Capitán, Duque de Alba* and *Don Juan de Austria* are located in Ceuta, Melilla and Fuerteventura, one of the Canary Islands. Their composition is two *banderas* or battalions, one mechanised and one motorised, plus an independent anti-tank company. The fourth *tercio, Alejandro Farnesio*, in Ronda, Málaga, has the *Grupo de Operaciones Especiales*, a cavalry *grupo* and training units.

One of the government's intentions appears to be the formation of a *Fuerza de Intervención Rápida* (a rapid intervention force), professional and ever-ready, and undoubtedly following the French pattern and sponsored by NATO. This force would include:

the Parachute Brigade and, possibly, the air-transportable one;

the *Tercio de Armada*, the Spanish Marines brigade-sized landing force;

the *Grupos de Operaciones Especiales*, as a specialised surprise attacking force;

the Foreign Legion. It is assumed that this contingent would be mainly the fourth *tercio*, since the other three have a more direct responsibility for the defence of their respective locations.

In fact, plans for a special voluntary service under a fixed salary were revealed in July 1986 and the first non-conscription units were precisely those above.

The Army Outside the Peninsula

No great changes due to the META plan have been reported for the units located in the two towns in northern Morocco and in both archipelagos. Ceuta and Melilla are the principal *foci* of tension in Spanish foreign policy, and the military forces located there are abnormally large. In order to keep the descriptions short, the approximate composition of the forces outside the Peninsula are shown in tabulated form:

CEUTA and MELILLA
Both towns have sensibly the same garrison, consisting of:
Headquarters company

Infantry:	One *tercio* of the Legion, one regiment of infantry of the line called '*regulares*' and formerly indigenous troops, with two *grupos* (battalions)
Cavalry:	one armoured regiment (M-48A5 tanks)
Artillery:	one regiment including self-propelled 155 mm howitzers and one light anti-aircraft *grupo* (35 mm Oerlikon guns)
Engineers:	one mixed regiment
Logistics:	one *agrupación* (regiment), including sanitary (medical) group, transport company and supply group
Other Forces:	one *Compañia de Mar* (sea operations), military police.

BALEARIC & CANARY ISLANDS
These constitute military zones independent from regions.

	Canary Islands	Balearic Islands
Headquarters	one company	one company
Infantry	5 battalions plus 2 armoured companies 1 *Tercio* of the Legion	2 battalions
Special Operations	1 company	1 company
Military Police	3 companies	3 companies
Cavalry	1 light group	1 light group
Artillery	2 mixed regiments, incl field, AA and probably coastal artillery	2 mixed regiments, incl field, AA and coastal artillery
Engineers	2 mixed battalions 1 signal battalion	1 mixed battalion Signal company or platoon
Logistics	Supply, transport and medical *grupos*	Supply, transport, medical *grupos* and veterinary unit
Air-Mobile	One general purpose unit	none

The above compositions might suffer in the next major changes, mainly in the reinforcement of the Islands' garrisons.

Cazacarros M-41 E TUA «Cazador»

Procurement Programmes

This article has been mainly devoted to describing organic organisational plans and to indicate the scope of the future Army. In fact, the reorganisation was completed for the experimental 3rd Military Region (Levante) in 1984 and for the 2nd (South) and 3rd (Central) during 1985/86. The 4th and 5th Regions (Pirenaic East and West) started their reorganisation in 1985, and 1986/88 will see the completion of changes for the 6th Region (Northwest), the only one not having a full division and where reorganisation is being undertaken slowly. By 1988, therefore, the structure will be fully developed; although it is possible that the programme for barrack accommodation will not be completed, since one of the aims of META has been to provide barracks outside urban areas. This change in distribution comes from the frequent accusation that Franco's large army was placed in the towns because it was intended for civil repression rather than defence against external aggression.

The present plans, which are already showing results, try to join all the units forming every brigade in the same place or *base*, where separate *acuartelamientos* (barracks) are allocated to independent regiments or battalions.

Equipment procurement is another challenge to the Spanish Army; although, since 1970, Spanish-manufactured equipment has been ordered in increasing quantities – mainly tactical vehicles and light weapons – the Army is not self-sufficient in many areas. To close this report, we will mention the action being taken to remedy these deficiencies.

Future Main Battle Tank

The Spanish tank inventory has always been small when compared with other European countries, because the Army's needs take account of the country's geography, which has many rough and mountainous areas where a heavily armoured regiment is not effective. The present inventory consists of 299 AMX-30, 164 M-48A5 and 375 M-47E tanks. All the American-originated tanks have had their power plants refurbished to M-60 standard; this operation, according to unofficial sources, has been successful for the M-48s, but unsatisfactory for the old M-47s, which have compatibility problems between their 'new' engines and their refurbished but fatigued hulls and suspensions. Thus all the M-48A5s have 105 mm guns and Hughes Mk 7 fire control systems, but only a limited number of M-47Es have received the British L7 105 mm gun. As well, the Army is not happy with the AMX-30 and is considering a modernisation process for the transmissions, the source of most problems.

The future Spanish MBT programme has a funding of some 130-150 billion pesetas to procure 400 tanks of high standard, but no final decision has yet been taken, because the Army has a very complex and accurate but slow system for competitive evaluation. The most probable choice is the Lince, a shortened and lightened West German Leopard 2 tailored to Spanish requirements, but the Italian OF-40 or the French AMX-40 might also be chosen. The existing AMX-30 fleet, used in the 1 and 3 Divisions, will be furbished on a more limited budget. This work will be done by either coupling a new power plant and transmission – even the same as that fitted to the M-47/48s – or, more simply, by updating to French AMX-30B2 standard. In any case, the Army does not intend to expand its total number of tanks, merely update its existing inventory.

Armoured Infantry Vehicles

With an inventory of 1196 M-113s (which probably includes a number of derivatives) the purchases programme has now changed to the Pegaso BMR-600, a fast wheeled vehicle which has good mobility performance, and which may be bought in similar numbers to the M-113 by the end of this decade. This would include a number of cavalry scout derivatives or VEC, some of which are now being fitted with 90 mm guns.

Artillery

The Spanish San Carlos company has developed a 155 mm 39 calibre howitzer, known as the SB 155/39. This is intended to replace the old 105/26 howitzers at brigade level and the American 155/23s at division level, and currently under study is a proposal to use the barrel and recoil system in the emplacements of the venerable 152 mm (6-in) coastal guns. A self-propelled derivative of the SB 155/39 is under development and would serve to improve armoured artillery in the existing mechanised units and even, at a later stage, to replace the M108/109 howitzers now in service.

Anti-aircraft Artillery

Two different programmes for short-range missile procurement were approved in recent years, and these

Left: **The Cazador M41E 'TOW under Armour' tank destroyer is a rebuilt M41 light tank with an improved TOW missile launcher.**

Below: The Teruel-2 140 mm Multiple Rocket Launcher mounted on a Pegaso 3050 truck.

Right: Engineer equipment, including bridging and hovercraft, seen on display.

Below right: A special 6 × 6 Pegaso vehicle used for water searching purposes by the unique *Regimiento de Ponteneros y Especialidades* (Bridging and Special Task Regiment) at Zaragoza.

65

will provide 18 Roland systems on AMX-30 hulls, and 13 Aspide systems. It is said that these weapons are to be deployed in southern hot spots, mainly with a view towards North Africa, but we wonder whether their number is not intended to give mobile anti-aircraft protection to brigades and divisions respectively. Probably the main defect in Spanish major units is their close range self-defence, since by now their only anti-aircraft weapons consist of a battalion of obsolete Bofors 40 mm L/70s at divisional level. A new Spanish-designed fire control system for these guns, the CEBEISPA Lince, is being evaluated by the Army. It is based on LPD-20 radar with associated laser range-finding and optronic tracking. If accepted, about 100

systems will be bought. Santa Barbara also has under design a self-propelled armoured anti-aircraft weapon of limited size, armed with a single 40 mm L/70 gun and based on the previously mentioned self-propelled howitzer. In addition, the well-known Meroka naval point defence system, still in prototype stage in its ground-based variation, might also become a useful short-range weapon.

Anti-tank Missiles

The army has limited numbers of Cobra and Milan plus HOT fitted to anti-tank MBB 105 helicopters, and so it has an urgent need for a new missile over the next few years, but this competition also appears to be going very slowly. News about a third-generation Spanish anti-tank missile named Toledo has given way to Spanish co-operation in the European future missile programme. Before this appears, perhaps the Army will choose a standardised missile of existing type, either Improved TOW or an European design.

Coastal Missiles

Plans for the procurement of coast-launched anti-ship missiles are in the early stages and the Army will probably evaluate Penguin, Harpoon, Exocet MM40 and Otomat. Should a truck-mobile system be approved, it will be used to improve the present coastal defence system, which in recent years has seen many reductions in older traditional equipment.

Helicopters

Several procurement programmes are under way, the most remarkable resulting in the purchase of 18 Super Puma machines for heavy transport. There are also plans to purchase general purpose helicopters to replace and increase existing numbers, as well as helicopters for mountain operation and for the Canary Islands.

Other Programmes

The electronic warfare programme has spread into universities, private companies and military-dependent facilities and its first achievements are the two EW battalions, one strategic, in the Regiment of RTM (*Red Territorial de Mando*) and special services, plus one tactical, in the Transmissions Regiment. Another programme will digitalise the RTM or communications network of the army. The second phase for EW provision is to be simultaneous with the procurement of enemy radar warning sets for Army helicopters, currently the subject of a competition between the Spanish CESELSA firm and Israeli companies.

Other minor programmes include an R&D one, under NATO co-operation, for a propulsion-assisted 155 mm shell, a PEPAD 105 mm shell, laser communications system, hypervelocity shells, electronic time fuzes, a microprocessor for communication encoding and decoding, and a multiple launcher vehicle.

This approach to the Spanish Army has been an attempt to predict the future organisation, with an additional look at equipment through the programmes which are in hand for the near future. The author hopes that this will have been helpful for those knowing the former organisation of the Spanish Army and also for those wishing to have a general overview of this fast-changing structure.

The Year in View

A gallery of things seen, announced, or in the news during 1986.

Above: **A Scammell Logistic Supply Vehicle with the DROPS (Demountable Rack Off-loading and Pick-up System) flatrack loaded with ammunition, demonstrating its ability at BAEE.** (*A.T. Hogg*)

Below: **'I think it went down there'. US Army M1 Abrams tank on exercises in Germany.** (*I.V. Hogg*)

Above left: **Vaime silent sniping rifles from Finland.** (*Oy Vainmenninmetalli AB*)

Left: **FH70 prepares to motor off under its own power after showing its paces at the BAEE firepower demonstration.** (*A.T. Hogg*)

Above: **A new method of tank-hunting? A remote-controlled chassis carrying a LAW-80 anti-tank rocket launcher, seen at BAEE.** (*A.T. Hogg*)

Left: **The Vickers AS90 155 mm self-propelled howitzer unveiled at BAEE. Could this replace SP70?** (*A.T. Hogg*)

Below left: **The Phoenix remotely piloted vehicle will shortly enter British Army service.** (*A.T. Hogg*)

Below: **A batch of Swedish FH-77B 155 mm howitzers under manufacture for the Indian Army.** (*AB Bofors*)

Left: **Rapier 2000, the updated version of the well-known air defence missile. A £1000 million order has been placed with British Aerospace for delivery of this system to the British Army in the mid-1990s. (***British Aerospace***)**

Top: **Colt celebrated their 150th anniversary this year, and announced the fact in some style at the AUSA show in Washington. (***A.T. Hogg***)**

Above: **The Göncz Assault pistol, an extremely high-quality weapon manufactured in the USA. (***A.T. Hogg***)**

Right: **The Chinese Type 83 155 mm self-propelled howitzer. (***Norinco***)**

Below: **Short's Starstreak air defence hyper-velocity missile has been selected as the next generation shoulder-fired weapon for the British Army. (***Short Brothers***)**

The British Aerospace Thunderbolt hyper-velocity air defence missile was developed to the same requirement as Starstreak but was not selected. It may yet have export potential. (*British Aerospace*)

Above: **The 'Andros Robot', developed in France for dealing with explosive devices, can tuck its tracks up to allow it to turn round in confined spaces. (*A.T. Hogg*)**

Below: **A model of the Rapier missile system fitted to an American Bradley infantry fighting vehicle, a suggestion put forward as an answer to the continuing American quest for a divisional air defence system. (*A.T Hogg*)**

ERSTA – a Lady to Respect

Terry Gander

Elsewhere in this edition of *Jane's Military Review* mention will be found of the coastal batteries established on Gibraltar 100 years ago. Although those batteries are still there they are now museum pieces for coastal defences were abandoned by the British defence establishment during the late 1950s. They felt, as many others did at the time, that the advent of the nuclear device and the potential power of strike aircraft meant that there was no longer any place for coastal defences – they were too vulnerable, lacking in potential power and quite simply no longer viable.

Many gunners who had experienced or used the power of coastal artillery voiced their doubts at the time but they were overruled. Those voices are now being heeded once again for the past decade has seen a resurgence in attention given to coastal defences of all kinds. The main reason for this has been the large increase in amphibious attack capability by the world's two major military powers. Both now have the potential to make large-scale amphibious landings on coastlines in any part of the world, coastlines that are in the main devoid of defences of even the most basic nature. So against all the forecasts of yesterday coastal defences are once more coming back into vogue.

This change-round has caused a feeling of quiet self-justification in one particular nation, namely Sweden. Along with several other Scandinavian and Baltic nations Sweden has never neglected its coastal defences – quite the reverse in fact, for while many other once well-defended nations ignored them, Swedes have been actively modernising and improving their shore defences over the years. They have maintained a well-manned and trained coastal defence organisation under the auspices of the Royal Swedish Navy and Swedish defence industries have continued to develop and produce weapons and equipment of all kinds especially for their coastal defences. The result is that Sweden is now the world leader in coastal defences, including coastal artillery and its organisation.

The reasons for this retention of a form of defence that most other nations have seen fit to ignore are not difficult to find. Sweden has a long coastline that is seemingly open to attack and many of its main centres of population and industry, along with their associated ports and harbours, are close to the sea. Any determined sea-borne invasion could take over the bulk of the Swedish infrastructure within a very short period but the Swedes have been aware of that likelihood for centuries. They have learned how to defend themselves and their chosen way of life, and are determined to carry on doing so for as long as they can. Thus the main potential foe, namely the Soviet Union and only a short distance away, is closely watched and defences are maintained to ensure that any attempt to invade any part of Sweden will meet with such a response that any aggressor's attempts would be counter-productive in terms of casualties, material losses and delays.

Thus long stretches of the Swedish coastline are defended by artillery batteries and other measures, both static and mobile. The static defences are the main point of concentration in this article for the Swedes have only rarely allowed any information relating to them to be known. To make their defensive stance fully effective they intend to keep any information relating to their defensive measures as discreet as they can to keep any potential enemy in the dark for as long as possible, despite the effectiveness of modern surveillance methods and satellite-carried cameras. They have succeeded to a surprising degree, and only recently have they allowed any information relating to one of their main coastal artillery equipments to be even printed.

Thus when the opportunity was offered for the author to make a visit to one of their coastal defence installations the offer was taken up with alacrity. The visit was to an ERSTA battery somewhere in the Stockholm archipelago. As was to be expected the actual location was not divulged and is still not known to me, even though I spent some time at the place, and I would certainly not be able to find it again.

This is due entirely to the Stockholm archipelago

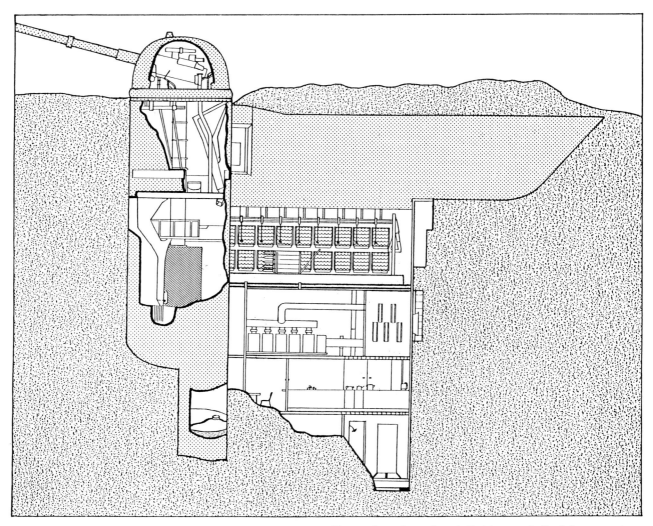

Above: **A schematic drawing of an ERSTA gun installation.**

itself. Like so much else of the Swedish coastline it consists of a vast number of small islands, rocks and shoals – in the Stockholm area there are about 24,000 small islands and skerries alone. To weave a way through this maze of islets is a major navigation feat but the locals know the area well – and so do some Soviet submariners for the area has been the subject of several Soviet mini-submarine forays in recent years. They have no doubt been involved in the clandestine surveillance of the local defences for the area is well provided with them.

For the Swedes coastal defence means not just coastal artillery. There are guided missile batteries, coastal ranger battalions, amphibious commando units, coastal patrol vessels, minelayers and minefields, both controlled and 'free standing', and the Royal Swedish Air

Force also takes a hand. Evidence of all of these can be seen if you know where to look on any journey around Sweden. Off shore there are also signs of coastal batteries from the past when rusting gun housings can be detected here and there. But to spot a modern coastal defence battery is well-nigh impossible without guidance.

Camouflage of the batteries is taken to considerable lengths and is made easier by the fact that only a minute portion of any installation is above ground surface. This is usually the turret and as well as being relatively easy to conceal, the turret also marks the major innovation introduced into modern static coastal artillery. The turret, or cupola, has for long been a major feature of fortification technique but its use in coastal defence has been rare in the past. Most coastal artillery was protected by barbettes or similar lightly-armoured gun housings and therefore vulnerable to air attack – any form of overhead protection usually limited barrel traverse. The turret not only allows a free traverse, it can be well armoured and thus remains a viable form of protection that is difficult to see and even a near miss will usually produce little damage. With ERSTA even a close detonation of a nuclear device will cause little, if any, damage and the gun will remain in action. Therefore the modern Swedish batteries are turret-based.

The first Swedish coastal gun in this category was a 75 mm weapon introduced in the 1960s although a few 152 mm turrets had been produced before then. These 75 mm guns and their turrets formed of 70 mm thick armour were produced in some numbers and many are still emplaced and in service today. Their installations contain underground ammunition magazines and an automatic feed system. The range of these guns is 12,000 metres.

These 75 mm guns were produced by AB Bofors and using the experience gained with them they were asked to produce a 120 mm turret gun. The result was introduced into service in 1976 and is what must be the most powerful gun in the world today, namely ERSTA.

ERSTA is a code name – I have yet to discover its 'proper' designation – but it is a name that demands respect. The name relates not just to the gun, although it is the main part of the weapon system, but to the complete installation, an installation that can only be described as massive for the guns are just the iceberg tips of structures that are buried deep in living rock. To construct such an installation is a major civil engineering achievement and usually involves blasting away masses of granite to make room for four- or five-storey underground structures that house not just the gun, its ammunition system and fire control facilities but living accommodation and the associated utilities that allow a gun crew to remain operational for months on end.

The battery I was shown consisted of a fire control centre and three ERSTA guns. Associated with the battery was a coastal ranger unit for local defence and a 120 mm mortar battery to provide fire cover in the event of a landing on any part of the battery. Each gun and the fire control centre were dotted about over an area covering several kilometres with each installation on a separate island. Direct contact between the installations is by small patrol or landing craft that would, in an emergency, ferry defenders and materials about as well.

A description of one ERSTA installation will suffice for them all although they vary slightly one from another. The fire control centre was visited first and entry was via a series of massive steel doors approached via steps cut into the rock. Above ground there was virtually nothing to see until one came across a huge flat T-shaped steel structure set into the surface. This was the protective cover for the fire control radar, a PEAB system known as the 9KA 400 KASTELL. When required, the steel covers are opened and the aerial is raised for use. It is not the only fire control system employed for there is also an optronic system with its window on the world hidden underneath what appears to be a rock. Close up, it can be seen to be a turret but

from even a few metres distance it merges into the surroundings and from a vessel it would be invisible. The turret houses a video camera and the usual optical surveillance devices, all protected behind a heavy steel sliding shutter.

The fire control centre has four floors. The 'basement' contains electrical generators, the water supply system and other utilities. It is also way below the level of the sea, not very far distant. Above are the crew's accommodation and the kitchens. The top two floors are the working areas with banks of radar monitors and the communication links with the other guns in the battery and to the rear. ERSTA hooks into an overall command and control network known as STRIKA and the interface units for this are also in the fire control centre.

A boat-ride away was one of the battery's ERSTA guns. This is somewhat more visible above ground than the fire control centre for the turret and barrel of ERSTA are not easy to conceal. When not in use the turret and gun are covered by irregular-shaped layers of an infra-red absorbent material that is coloured and shaped to resemble the surrounding rocky terrain. Thus although the covers stand out at close range they are impossible to spot from a distance. To conceal them further dummy installations are established near some batteries and use may be made of camouflage netting.

When entering an ERSTA installation one is immediately reminded of the old French 'Maginot Line' forts. There is the same approach into the ground and the same array of thick steel doors. Each set of doors acts as a seal against the world outside, culminating in an NBC decontamination room, complete with showers and changing facilities, before the main interior is reached. As in the fire control centre the entire installation is joined by a common spiral stairway that serves each floor – in a gun installation there are five floors. Again the 'basement' houses the water puri-fication and electrical equipment, and the floor above is the main living and eating area. The floors above are the working areas and once again there is a fire control room, this time with a purely local function in case of a communication loss with the main fire control centre.

The main impression gained when looking around the installation was that everything was ready for a crew to walk in and commence work. The kitchens were spotless with eating utensils and cooking equipment laid out ready for instant use. In the fire control room not only were maps and range tables laid out in their working positions but even a full complement of pencils and thumb-tacks were correctly stowed in their appointed places. The battery visited was empty, ready for its reservist and conscript crew to move in for their regular training periods or for the real thing in an emergency – everything was in place, ready to use and kept so by regular maintenance visits and a dry air system that maintains a constant internal temperature and humidity.

This was particularly evident in the gun-associated

Above: **An ERSTA turret hidden under its camouflage cover.**
(*Terry Gander*)

Right: **The optronic fire control turret located at an ERSTA fire control centre with the shutter seen firmly closed.** (*Terry Gander*)

part of the installation and at this point some information relating to the 120 mm ERSTA gun is necessary. It has already been stated that ERSTA is the most powerful gun in the world today and a sight of it demonstrates why. It is massive. The barrel alone is over seven metres long and the turret armour is over 70 mm thick – the turret stands higher than a man. Underground are two storeys of magazine and ammunition feed system.

What ERSTA cannot normally show is its firepower. It can fire up to 25 rounds a minute and in a period of 20 minutes can fire off 200 rounds. Needless to say the barrel has to be water-cooled using water from a sump at the base of the tubular centre-structure that is pumped through a barrel jacket. Each shell weighs 24 kg and the maximum range at present is 27,000 metres – enhanced

range ammunition is in the development pipeline and there is talk of some form of corrected-trajectory round. Most rounds used are what are termed naval target shells fitted with delayed-action fuzes that detonate the shell only after it has penetrated the target's armour. The other type of round is a streamlined naval target shell with an improved explosive payload – it can be fitted with a base bleed unit for even more range. This shell is known as a high capacity enhanced range or HCER. Accuracy is stated to be excellent, to the point where at intermediate ranges the point of contact on a target such as a large naval vessel can be selected and hit.

The gun crew is eleven men: fire commander, two layers, seven ammunition numbers and a gun mechanic. The seven ammunition handlers work in the magazine room, known to all as the Chapel. It is a high-roofed chamber with ammunition stacked in pallets around the walls. The pallets can be handled using overhead rails or trolleys mounted on rollers and there is stated to be enough ammunition in the Chapel for three major engagements. The ammunition handlers move the pallets to a transfer table and load the fixed rounds onto it. From the table the rounds are automatically fed horizontally into an X-shaped device that realigns them vertically and sends them along a hoist on their way upwards to the gun itself. At the top of the feed system the rounds are swung out into a rotary magazine that holds the rounds ready to be fed into a pendulum device to the rammer. From there they are automatically

Above: **The radar room inside a fire control centre with the video monitor from the optronic system mounted over the screens.** (*Terry Gander*)

Above right: **The huge T-shaped steel cover for the KASTELL fire control radar aerial.** (*Terry Gander*)

Right: **A KASTELL aerial coming into the raised position.** (*AB Bofors*)

rammed into the chamber for firing. Ramming can be carried out at any angle of barrel elevation.

Looking throughout the central tube structure that carries the turret and the ammunition feed system it is easy to see why a gun mechanic is needed. The whole set-up resembles a large and complex central heating installation with pipes and wiring seemingly everywhere. After even a little guidance it all makes sense and following a clamber up and down the ladder to the turret it all fits into place. The turret interior is crammed with fire control gear, all of the follow-the-pointer type. The two layers are seated one each side of the gun and are separated from the gun mechanism by windows that cut out virtually all sounds of operation including, apparently, the actual firing noise. The gun commander

is also in the turret overseeing the layers and making use of a roof-mounted periscope that provides a small degree of fire control to be carried out from the gun itself. Spent propellant cases are routed down the central tube to the sump at the base.

Some of the details of an ERSTA installation can only be seen when the ERSTA equipments are examined on the AB Bofors production line at Karlskoga. These days the production rate is two guns a year, which in itself provides an idea of the scale of an ERSTA installation, but today the customer is Norway. After many years of service the old Second World War guns (often of German origin) dotted around Norway are being replaced in some areas by ERSTAs. In various ways the Norwegian ERSTAs are even more advanced than the Swedish weapons for they make use of laser rangefinding as part of their optronic fire control systems. Each complete equipment is partially assembled at the factory for testing and then broken down into its component parts for delivery. It takes no less than 18 railway flat-cars to carry just one ERSTA to its destination in Norway.

This description cannot impart any sense of the state of preparedness of a Swedish coastal artillery ERSTA installation. The mere sight of the racks of ammunition stacked ready for genuine use drives home the real meaning of a defensive stance and everywhere the high level of cleanliness and serviceability gives an impression that ERSTAs *will* be used if the need arises. The initial 'Maginot Line' impression engendered by visits to the remaining French forts soon fades when one realises that ERSTA fulfils a valid and modern defensive function and that the ERSTA batteries have been emplaced to make sure that one small nation remains apart from the major power struggles taking place elsewhere. A visit certainly forces home the impression that ERSTA is a lady to respect.

Acknowledgements
The author would like to express his thanks to the personnel from AB Bofors and The Royal Vaxholms Coastal Artillery Regiment (KA1) who made possible a unique experience. I only hope that they find the above article worthy of their efforts.

Left: **The ammunition transfer table in the magazine ('Chapel') of an ERSTA installation. (***Terry Gander***)**

Below left: **The ammunition racks inside the ERSTA magazine. (***AB Bofors***)**

Below: **The NBC decontamination room outside the main entrance to an ERSTA installation showing showers ready for use. (***Terry Gander***)**

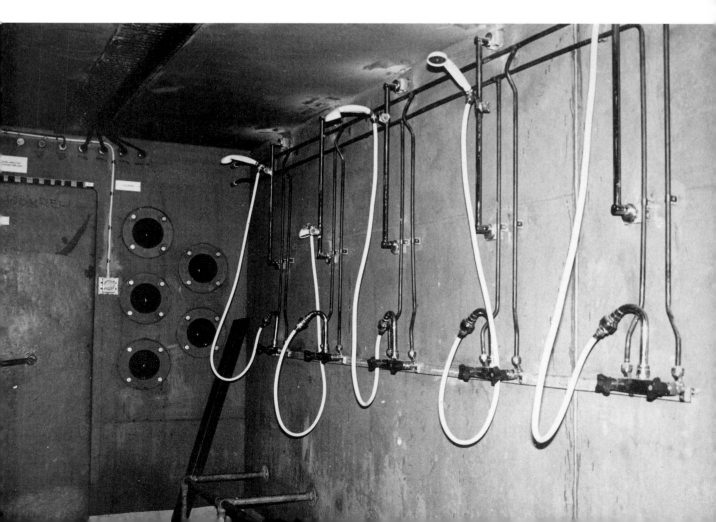

Above: **Part of the water purfication plant in the deep basement of an ERSTA installation.** (*Terry Gander*)

The Mortar in the Eighties

Charles Castle

The position of the mortar varies among armies; at one end of the scale some regard it as a light artillery weapon and treat it with respect, at the other end it is considered to be no more than an overgrown grenade thrower best left alone. In general, continental armies have tended towards the upper end of the scale, western armies towards the lower, but there seems to be an air of change in the offing.

Light mortars, of 60 mm to 82 mm calibre, have long been accepted as useful adjuncts to the infantry platoon or company in all armies. The medium mortar, of 120 mm calibre, has been adopted widely among European armies since 1945, largely due to German and Soviet experience with this calibre during the Second World War, but it has seen very little recognition from the British or American armies until now. This is not to say that it has never been contemplated; the British Army tested the rifled Hotchkiss-Brandt 120 mm mortar in the early 1960s, but without coming to any firm conclusions, and even before that the Royal Armaments Research & Development Establishment had developed a 4.5-inch (114 mm) mortar to an advanced stage in the mid-1950s. This latter idea was abandoned on a change of policy, and it was probably the lingering effects of this policy which negated the Brandt design.

In 1983, however, the Canadian Army began to show an interest in a medium mortar and purchased a number of Brandt 120 mm rifled models. This was followed by the US Marines obtaining some Tampella 120 mm mortars from Finland and, it is believed, conducting tests on the Brandt rifled weapon. In 1986 the Royal Ordnance Factory announced a new breech-loading 120 mm mortar for fitting into light armoured vehicles, and rumours now suggest that the British Army is showing an interest in a conventional ground-platform 120 mm mortar and intends to hold trials of various patterns in the near future.

What seems to have precipitated this interest is the recent development of more sophisticated projectiles for this class of weapon. Heretofore the mortar has been characterised by relatively cheap bombs which relied for their effect on blast and fragmentation, augmented by their steep angle of descent which ensured a wide and all-round distribution of fragments. These were perfectly adequate for the routine anti-personnel role of the mortar, but it was because of this common-place application that armies tended to neglect the medium calibre, particularly, as in the case of the British and American armies, where they had well-integrated close artillery support.

Artillery support was often preferred to mortars because of the ability of artillery to deliver airburst fire against targets behind cover, but this advantage has now been whittled away by the widespread adoption of proximity fuzes for mortar bombs. The cheapness and reliability of solid-state electronics can now produce a proximity/point detonating fuze which is little more expensive than a traditional mechanical impact fuze and which, by a simple adjustment, can be set to burst on impact or at some optimum height above the ground, so showering the target area with high velocity fragments. Given this ability and a substantial bomb, the infantry mortar yields nothing to the artillery gun or howitzer in effectiveness.

It is the promise of munitions with rather more potential than a simple explosion which gives the medium mortar a more versatile role. The first suggestion which springs to mind is, of course, the anti-armour bomb fitted with a seeking head. There are a number of designs of guided mortar bomb under development, and the 120 mm calibre is attractive to the designer if for no better reason than that it has more space inside it for the guidance mechanism and yet still leaves room for a satisfactory explosive payload. A 120 mm calibre shaped charge warhead descending onto the upper surfaces of a tank will most certainly put the tank out of action permanently, and the average medium mortar should be able to fire such a projectile to a range of five or six kilometres with relative ease. Guidance

and 4300 m respectively. The sub-munitions are small shaped charge bomblets with a fragmenting sleeve around the charge so that they have both anti-armour and anti-personnel effect. Each bomblet delivers about 650 fragments, will penetrate 150 mm of armour and has a lethal radius of eight metres. The bomblets are distributed from the parent bomb by an airburst fuze, and depending upon the height of burst the bomblets can cover an area up to 4000 square metres.

It should be emphasised that there is no question of guidance in these bombs; the mortar is fired in the usual manner, but the bursting of the bomb distributes the bomblets so as to cover an area beneath with sub-munitions, some of which will surely find targets. Bearing in mind the rate of fire that a skilled mortar squad can produce – 12 to 15 rounds per minute is the usual figure for this calibre – it can be seen that a burst of fire from four mortars would produce a high degree of saturation of a target area.

Left: **The Yugoslavian M74 120 mm light mortar, together with its rocket-boosted bomb.**

Above: **A typical proximity/point detonating mortar fuze, the Norwegian Kongsberg PPD-323.**

Right: **The Spanish Espin 21 (*left*) and Espin 15 (*right*) sub-munition bombs.**

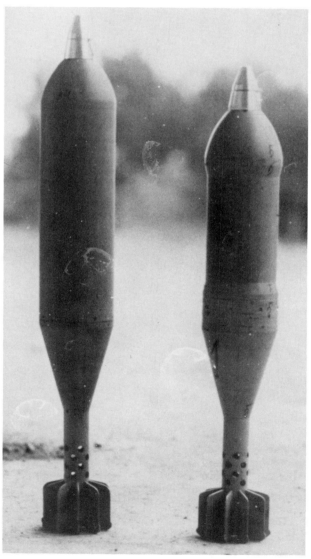

systems which have been suggested include millimetric wave radar and infra-red homing, and both these techniques are sufficiently well advanced to hold out the prospect of having bombs in service by the end of the present decade.

More recently, however, the medium mortar bomb has been developed as a means of delivering sub-munitions. This idea was first heard of about three years ago as a possibility, and in 1986 three different designs have been announced. Esperanza y Cia of Spain, a long-established company specialising in mortars, produced two bombs known as 'Espin', the name deriving from Esperanza's collaboration with another Spanish company, Instalaza SA. Espin is a parallel-walled bomb containing a number of small sub-munitions: Espin 15 carries 15 bomblets, Espin 21 carries 21 bomblets and the two types range to 5500 m

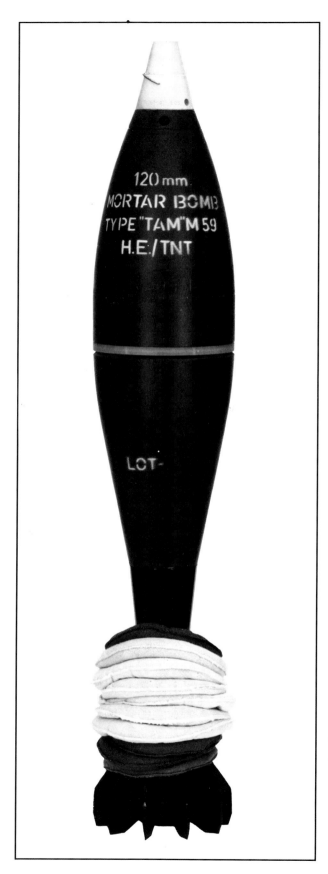

The next design to be announced was the Pyrkal GRM-20, developed by the Greek Powder & Cartridge Company of Athens. This bomb has been developed for the ex-American 4.2-inch (107 mm) M2 and M30 mortars with which the Greek Army is equipped. This is a rifled mortar, firing a projectile with parallel walls which resembles an artillery shell by having a driving band; this is under bore diameter when loaded at the muzzle but is expanded by the explosion of the propelling charge so as to engage in the rifling as the bomb leaves the barrel. The shape of the bomb gives the maximum space for the calibre, and there are no less than 20 sub-munitions inside it. Each of these bomblets is fitted with a dragline stabiliser and an impact fuze, and is loaded with a shaped charge capable of penetrating 60 mm of armour. As with the Espin bomb, the shaped charge is surrounded by a fragmentation sleeve which gives an anti-personnel effect around the point of impact. The parent bomb can be fitted with a time or proximity fuze so as to burst it over the target area, and the sub-munitions are scattered in a circle with a radius of about 200 metres.

The most recent design to be announced is one from the Royal Ordnance Factories, introduced at the same time as the breech-loading mortar referred to above. No details of the contents or performance have yet been made public, but the bomb is a conventional finned type for firing from smooth-bores, and it might be expected to be similar to the Espin design in its essentials.

Looking ahead, there seems to be no reason why sub-munition bombs containing anti-personnel mines should not be developed as the next step. The infantry mortar company would then have the ability to deny possible approach or concentration areas at long range and establish a system of barriers designed to channel any attack into predetermined lanes. These lanes could then be covered by anti-personnel bomblets as well as conventional mortar bombs, and any accompanying armour could also be brought under attack. A medium mortar complete with this range of ammunition can provide a total defensive system.

Defence, though, is only part of warfare, and the offensive must also be studied. The sub-munition bombs have their applications in this role as well, but a more useful projectile for offensive tasks is the extended-range bomb. Analysis of a number of conventional 120 mm mortars firing ordinary bombs gives us an average bomb-weight of 13.5 kg and an

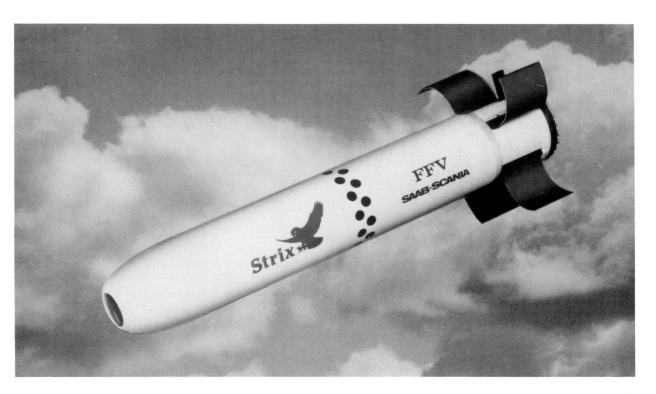

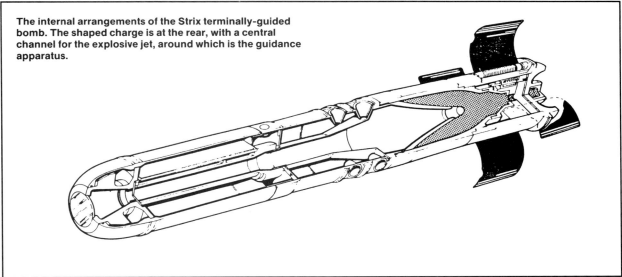

The internal arrangements of the Strix terminally-guided bomb. The shaped charge is at the rear, with a central channel for the explosive jet, around which is the guidance apparatus.

average maximum range of 6850 m. There are two ways of improving this performance, both of which are adopted by different armies. Firstly, the use of a lighter bomb with a better ballistic shape, and secondly the addition of rocket propulsion to the bomb.

The former type is usually identified simply as a 'long-range bomb'. It is usually somewhat smaller and lighter than the standard bomb, uses a better grade of steel and a more brisant high explosive so as to ensure good fragmentation from the reduced payload, and is well-shaped and provided with an efficient obturating ring which ensures that as much as possible of the

propelling gas actually works on the bomb and does not leak past it in the barrel of the mortar. The increase in range due to these measures varies greatly; some long range bombs give an improvement of about 10 per cent of range, others can show as much as 27 per cent. The difference is generally due to the parent mortar, those with longer barrels showing the better increase due to generating a higher muzzle velocity.

Rocket assistance is not widely used; in the mortar field it was pioneered by Brandt, who developed the 120 mm PEPA rocket-boosted bomb in the 1960s. This gave a range increase of 54 per cent over the standard

Left: **A smoke bomb for the American 107 mm mortar. It can be seen that the high-capacity shape makes this a good design for converting into a sub-munition bomb, as has been done in Greece.**

Right: **The PRPA rocket-boosted bomb used with the French Brandt 120 mm rifled mortar.**

bomb, though it should be said that at that time the maximum range of the standard Brandt 120 mm mortar was only 4250 m. An increase of range to 8000 m was substantial, but since that time conventional designs of mortar and bomb have bettered even the rocket-assisted range. Brandt responded to these improvements by developing a strengthened mortar which added another 1000 m to the maximum range, and they then produced a rocket-boosted bomb for their rifled 120 m mortar. In standard form the rifled mortar can fire a 16 kg conventional bomb to a range of 8135 m, and the PRPA (Projectile Raye a Propulsion Additionelle) rocket-boosted bomb extends this to 13 km, a percentage increase of almost 60 per cent.

The prinicpal objection voiced to rocket-boosted bombs is that the inclusion of a rocket motor takes away space from the interior of the bomb and thus reduces the payload. The Israeli rocket-boosted 120 mm bomb weighs 16.7 kg as loaded and carries an explosive payload of 2.15 kg of Composition B, so that the payload/weight ratio is 12.8 per cent. By comparison, the conventional bomb for the same mortar weighs 13.2 kg as loaded and carries 2.3 kg of TNT, a ratio of 17.5 per cent. The actual reduction in payload, due to the somewhat different shapes of the two bombs, is relatively small but the percentage difference is more significant.

A lesser objection is that of reduced accuracy. The operation of a rocket-boosted bomb is such that the bomb is fired from the mortar and the rocket is ignited, after a short delay, during the bomb's upward flight. This accelerates the bomb so that the velocity increases and the vertex of the trajectory is moved to a point higher and further away from the mortar. The rocket is all-burnt before vertex, and the bomb thereafter continues its flight in an entirely ballistic mode, just as it would have done had it been launched initially at the higher velocity. The objection to this is that when the rocket ignites, the bomb may well be yawing in flight. The amount of yaw exhibited by a fin-stabilised mortar bomb during the first few hundred feet of flight is astonishing: variations of up to 40 degrees from the axis of the trajectory are not uncommon, but the design of the bomb, with fins at the end of a tail boom, is such that this movement is rapidly damped down and the bomb soon settles on its planned course. But should it, for any

Loading the Brandt 120 mm mortar.

Above: **Ammunition for the Spanish Ecia 120 mm mortar:
second from the left is the standard high explosive bomb, and
third from the right is the long range bomb, showing the
difference in ballistic shaping.**

reason, still be yawing when the rocket motor fires, then it will be driven off its trajectory in the direction of the yaw. And depending upon which direction the axis of the bomb is oriented at that instant, so the range may be slightly increased or decreased, and there will probably be some element of azimuthal displacement.

What this means in practice is that the Circle of Probable Error around the mean point of impact will be somewhat increased. Actual figures are impossible to come by, but it seems fairly safe to say that whatever the CPE of a conventional bomb, a rocket-assisted bomb will double it.

However, too much can be made of this. The mortar, we are always told, is an area weapon, and the fire of four 120 mm mortars at 8 km range using rocket-assisted bombs would still be sufficiently accurate for all practical purposes.

There is, though, another aspect of long range mortar fire which must be considered. For the past 30 or more years we have been assured that the day of the mortar is over because of mortar-locating radars, which can detect a bomb in flight and compute the position of the mortar before the bomb has even reached its target. And having been actively engaged in the development and operation of mortar-locating radars for many years, I will support this statement. So there seems to be some conflict in progress; on the one hand the radar experts assuring us that no mortar will go unpunished, and on the other hand the mortar specialists devising more and better bombs to fire to longer ranges.

I do not pretend to know the official answer to this, having been long retired from the radar business, but I suspect it to rest on practical grounds; that there will rarely be a solitary mortar firing (the radar operator's ideal case) and that in the hurly-burly of the battlefield it will be possible to deliver mortar fire which will be lost to radars in the general confusion. That and, probably, the deployment of active countermeasures may well have diminished the mortar-locating radar's threat value. I might add that 'stealth' technology – mortar bombs invisible to radar – were tried about 25 years ago and found to be impractical.

One further problem facing the adoption of heavier mortars is that of controlling the fire. In the days of short-range mortars they were controlled in a very rudimentary fashion, frequently from the mortar position itself since the target could be easily seen. But with ranges of 8 to 10 km in prospect, this no longer applies and it begins to look as if the mortar company must base itself on artillery practice and deploy observers, set up a communications system, have a command post to process the observer's data and control the weapons, and generally place an organisational infra-structure on and about the four tubes on the ground. In the past it has been the need for this infra-structure which has inhibited infantry from whole-hearted acceptance of medium and heavy

Modern mortar fire control: the radio operator is receiving corrections from an observer and producing data for the mortar on the small computer resting on the vehicle. The mortar commander uses another hand-held computer to check the figures.

Above: **The Soviet 160 mm mortar in travelling order. The towing attachment is clipped to the muzzle, and the wheels remain on the mount when in action.**

mortars, since the infantry are always short of manpower and prefer to see men carrying rifles rather than maps and compasses. But the general adoption of simple hand-held digital computers for solving the various gunnery problems can probably streamline the organisation and do away with the need for a command post, and provided NCOs are instructed in simple observing techniques the common radio network will suffice for sending fire orders back to the mortars. Improved communications and electronic aids look like being the means of adapting medium mortars to the current infantry organisation without having to burden it with additional unproductive manpower.

The prospect of firing mortar bombs to a range of 10 km can be very easily misconstrued: very few infantry commanders are particularly interested in what is happening 10 km away, though the ability to fire to this range does permit defensive fire plans to be set up in considerable depth in some circumstances. What is more important is that once the mortar is emplaced it can stay where it is during a fairly sizeable advance by forward troops. In the days when 4 km was the maximum range, the mortar would have to be uprooted and redeployed fairly rapidly and fairly often during the advance; now it can stay in place for a far longer time and still have the ability to respond to calls for fire from the advancing troops. An additional attraction to having a

long-range weapon is that it permits a greater latitude in siting within one's own lines, while retaining the same amount of command in front. A weapon with a 4 km maximum range, and requiring to engage targets up to 3 km from the front line, has but a 1 km deep belt of countryside in which to find a position. A mortar with an 8 km maximum range, covering the same depth into the enemy's area, will have the ability to move around in a 5 km deep area to find a position without jeopardising his primary tasks.

Will mortars increase in size? I doubt it. The Soviets, as we know, use a 160 mm mortar, and the Finns and Israelis also use this calibre. The Soviet M-160 fires a 41.5 kg bomb to a range of 8040 m, and has a rate of fire of two to three rounds per minute. It is a breech-loaded weapon of some complexity but is probably cheaper to manufacture than a comparable howitzer and is certainly, at 1650 kg, lighter than any conventional gun or howitzer of the same calibre would be. The Finnish and Israeli mortars have much in common, firing a 40 kg bomb to 10,000 metres range. The bomb is loaded at the muzzle, necessitating lowering the barrel after every shot, and the barrel is fitted with a counterweight system to make this easier. Even so, one is inclined to feel that the maker's claim to a rate of fire of 8 rounds per minute applies only to extremely fit, well-built and well-trained crews. In the firing position, the mortar weighs 1700 kg.

It is difficult to see what these weapons can do that conventional howitzers cannot do better. Their only advantage lies in their economy, since the advantage of weight is of little consequence. For those reasons it is unlikely that the 160 mm mortar will gain any further adherents, leaving 120 mm as the topmost calibre. And with the tactical gains which stem from the new types of ammunition, there seems to be a bright future ahead for the medium mortar.

Above: **The Finnish Tampella 160 mm mortar. Note how the wheels are arranged so as to assist in traversing the mortar for direction. The front support strut hinges so as to lower the barrel for loading.**

Below: **One more advantage of the 120 mm mortar: it can be helicopter-lifted to bring in rapid fire support.**

Not So Secret Weapons

The Second World War saw a huge number of developments in equipment which, for one reason or another, never achieved service adoption and have since been forgotten. Another raid on our archives has produced this collection of what might have been.

Above: **Not the barrack fire-engine, but the 'Ladder, Scaling, 100-foot, 3-ton Ford' of 1943. The idea was to drive this ashore from a landing craft, dash to the bottom of the cliffs, erect the ladder, and thus enable the raiding party or invading troops to get to the cliff-top with less exertion than by using ropes. Finally abandoned as being impractical.**

Below: **Forget the Soviet 85 mm gun; this was the first auxiliary-propelled gun. The 17 pr (76.2 mm) anti-tank gun fitted with an extra wheel and a truck engine by Nicholas Straussler, the man who invented the swimming tank. Note that it could also pull its own ammunition trailer. The idea, developed in 1944, failed solely because of the enormous size of pit necessary to conceal it in action.**

Above: **If you thought the jeep was small, meet the British 'airborne tractor' developed in 1944 to pull a mortar (as here) or a 6 pr (57 mm) anti-tank gun. Made by Morris Motors, the idea was abandoned.**

Below: **The barrel of 'Little David', a 36-in (915 mm) calibre rifled muzzle-loading mortar firing a 1300 lb (590 kg) shell. Developed in the USA for demolishing Japanese fortifications, the war ended before its acceptance trials were completed.**

Above: A Canadian effort: the 3.7-in (94 mm) anti-aircraft gun mounted on top of a Sherman tank chassis. Judging by this picture the idea was to make it into a tank destroyer, but other pictures show the gun at 85 degree elevation, so it may have been a dual-purpose weapon. Whatever the purpose, it failed to impress the military.

Below: A 25 pr gun with the 'Vauxhall Wheel'. Developed by Vauxhall Motors, this was a steel wheel with a leather 'tyre' intended to economise on rubber. On trial it collapsed after 30 miles and 'every bolt on the gun carriage was loosened by the vibration.' The idea was abandoned.

Above: Another potential tank destroyer, the 17 pr Thorneycroft Carrier. This was a commercial truck encased in armour and with a 17 pr (76.2 mm) anti-tank gun pointing out from the rear. The idea probably began with the similar use of a 6 pr (57 mm) gun on trucks in the Western Desert, but the firing shock of a 17 pr was somewhat more violent, and the idea was dropped.

Above right: King Kong, or the Howitzer Motor Carriage T92, an American equipment which mounted the 240 mm howitzer on a special tracked chassis based on the T26 heavy tank. Approved in March 1945, 144 were ordered but only five had been built when the war ended and the contracts were immediately cancelled.

Right: Another Canadian idea, the 25 pr MARC (Mobile Armoured Redoubt, Canadian). This was a 25 pr (87.6 mm) gun mounted in an armoured turret on wheels. Everybody agreed it was a clever idea, but nobody agreed on how it ought to be used. So it didn't get used at all.

Above: **This cumbersome beast might have been the British heavy gun: a 6-inch (152 mm) of 45 calibres length, it was tested in 1941/42, but fortunately the American 155 mm Gun M1 came along to fill the gap.**

Below: **Another airborne idea was the British Alecto self-propelled 95 mm howitzer. This one might have reached service had the 95 mm howitzer been more successful, but 'teething troubles' delayed it so long that it was eventually abandoned.**

Below: **A foul day 'somewhere in England' and three intrepid testers put an experimental Rolls-Royce carrier through its paces early in 1945.**

Above: **One of the unsolved problems of the war was the provision of an 'intermediate' anti-aircraft gun, one which filled the gap between the 40 mm Bofors and the heavier weapons such as the British 3.7-inch (94 mm), the German 88 mm and the American 90 mm. Everybody tried, nobody succeeded. This is the British attempt, a twin 57 mm with an automatic loading mechanism which took up more space than the guns.**

A Return to the Gun?

Owen Carrow

The question of defeating armour is still one which occupies many minds in design establishments throughout the world, and the current roster of missiles and shoulder-fired rockets continues to grow. So far as performance goes there seems to be very little to choose between them, and the principal design effort seems to be aimed at producing the smallest possible weapon compatible with doing some worthwhile damage.

Unfortunately, size and performance do not go hand-in-hand. All things being equal, the weapon with the biggest warhead is obviously likely to have the best penetrative performance, but by the same token the odds are that the weapon with the biggest warhead will have poor flight characteristics and thus will not be able to fly at high velocity, or for long ranges, or with outstanding accuracy beyond a fairly limited distance. As a result we are now moving into a period where the options have polarised into three distinct solutions. Firstly there is the second-generation wire-guided missile, such as Milan or TOW; then comes what we might call the 'intermediate' man-carried rocket, exemplified by LAW 80 and Apilas, large and powerful in order to reach out as far as is commensurate with man-portability. And finally we have the lightweight shoulder-fired rockets of the type pioneered by the 66 mm M72 LAW and now exemplified by such weapons as Armbrust, Lanze, and the many M72-clones which have appeared in recent years.

These have their uses, there can be no doubt of that, but they all have their drawbacks as well. Principal among these drawbacks is the bulk of the missile systems and particularly of their reloads; the bulk of the intermediate systems, which don't have reloads; and hence the need to keep up a constant resupply of missiles and of the intermediate and short-range prepacked launchers so that the soldier is always ready for the appearance of enemy armour.

There is also the point that this three-way split leaves an area in the defensive plan which is capable of being covered only by the missile. Artillery remotely-delivered munitions and tank artillery can deal with armour at long ranges; the missiles come into their own at about 3 km from the line of resistance, but they are then the sole arbiters until the approaching armour gets within about 400 mm of the defences, when the intermediates and later the short-range launchers can join in. It would be nice if something could be made available to thicken up the missile defence in that critical 400 m to 2 km area, since the missile operators are obviously going to have their hands full if confronted with a full-scale armoured thrust.

It seems to be this sort of argument which has been responsible for a revival of interest in the 'cannon solution', the provision of specialised artillery with the primary task of combatting armour, and the secondary task of acting as direct support for infantry. But at this point a third factor has been added to the problem: the helicopter.

While the helicopter was no more than a battlefield runabout, nobody paid a great deal of attention to it as a potential target; if it got within range, yes, then machine guns would be pointed vaguely at it, although in practice helicopters are strangely difficult to shoot down in this manner. But now that the helicopter is becoming a weapons platform for the attack of tanks and ground troops, it has suddenly become a high priority to produce something capable of dealing with it. Various companies have developed missiles and light air defence guns with proximity fuzes optimised to respond to the peculiar echoes from the helicopter rotors, but most of these weapons are in the hands of specialised troops and are unlikely to be available to the front-line soldier. So in addition to the tank and general support role, the attack of helicopters has been added to the tasks for an infantry gun.

For those unfamiliar with the rise and fall of the anti-tank gun, a few background details might be of value. At the start of the Second World War most countries had light guns in the 37-40 mm calibre range, capable of being pushed around by two or three men and

easily concealed, and which were capable of damaging most of the tanks of 1939. But from 1940 onwards the tanks gradually became better protected and carried heavier guns, so that these small weapons were both out-ranged and incapable of piercing their opponent's armour. As a result, a second generation of weapons with calibres from 50 mm to 75 mm came along, to which the riposte was thicker armour and bigger tanks. At the close of the war weapons of 94 mm (UK), 105 mm (USA) and 128 mm (Germany) were being perfected so as to deal with the current and forthcoming tanks.

At the same time, the mechanics of armour penetration had undergone radical changes. At the beginning of the war plain steel shot, or steel piercing shell with a minuscule explosive charge, were the standard projectiles. As the tanks grew thicker and the armour became harder, so the projectiles changed, adopting tungsten carbide penetrating cores and carrying them in a variety of ways, culminating in the APDS (armour piercing, discarding sabot) projectile introduced by Britain in 1944. Tungsten was adopted because it was the only material capable of surviving the impact with armour in a condition to penetrate, and in order to do so it required high velocity. To achieve this the propelling charges grew bigger and bigger, and the guns, perforce, had to grow bigger and bigger in order to fire these massive cartridges.

The combination of increasing calibre and velocity meant that by 1945 the developmental guns mentioned above were in the range of seven to ten tons weight. No longer was it possible for their detachments to push them around, and concealment was a major problem. With the end of the war came the general embracement of recoilless guns firing shaped charge or squash-head shell, promising ample destructive power but low velocity and light weight, and the conventional anti-tank gun had almost disappeared by the early 1950s, except in Warsaw Pact countries.

The technology of the conventional gun did not, though, disappear. It was merely transferred to the tank gun, and the gradual improvement in ammunition which might have been expected had the anti-tank gun survived actually took place in the development of tank

ammunition, which led to smoothbore guns and the APFSDS (armour piercing, fin-stabilised, discarding sabot) projectile.

The tank gun crept up to 120 mm in calibre; there were one or two aberrant designs of greater calibre, but in general 120 mm has been accepted as the practical maximum, and for this you require a fairly substantial tank. In the past decade there has been a good deal of work done in developing lighter tanks, particularly with rapid deployment forces and airborne transportation in mind, which, in turn, has led to work on smaller calibre tank guns in the 75–90 mm bracket. Although the calibre has decreased, applying the latest ammunition technology has enabled these guns to retain credibility as a threat to the modern main battle tank. Firing APFSDS at high velocity, even a 75 mm gun can do severe damage at long range.

Having thus developed lightweight guns, the next logical step was to think about putting them on to wheeled carriages so that, once more, they could be pushed around the battlefield by a handful of men and concealed behind any convenient bush. The only problem here was to convince the soldiers of their validity as an anti-tank weapon. What you don't have, you don't miss, as the old saying has it, and soldiers unaccustomed to anti-tank guns are going to take some persuading.

To assist in this persuasion, manufacturers and designers are now pointing to the helicopter and to the infantry fighting vehicle and all the other light armoured machinery abounding on the battlefield, and suggesting that deployment of expensive missiles to deal with these threats is economic nonsense when a light and cheap gun can do the job equally well. Moreover a round of ammunition for one of these guns is generally no larger, if as large as, a reload for a missile or a replacement one-shot launcher, so that the logistics are not being strained, and in any case a gun will carry more ammunition with it than a missile will carry reloads.

The trend towards light infantry guns might be said to have been begun by the Belgian firm Mecar, who took a light 90 mm gun developed for mounting in armoured vehicles and placed it on a wheeled carriage. This has three stabiliser legs which spread, lifting the wheels from the ground, so that the weapon can be swiftly traversed through a complete circle and can easily follow moving targets. The whole equipment weighs only 880 kg and can be towed behind a light vehicle or even pulled by a handful of men quite easily. Ammunition provided for the anti-armour role is a shaped charge shell capable of penetrating about 375 mm of armour, and there is also an anti-personnel projectile with a range of 3 km, a smoke shell, and a canister shot for close-in defence. This gun has been adopted in some numbers by the Italian, West German and Swiss armies.

The next move came from Israel, where Israel Military Industries similarly took a gun originally developed for vehicular mounting and turned it into a field piece. The 60 mm HVMS (hyper-velocity medium support) gun was originally designed to be fitted to such vehicles as the M113 APC, so giving a cheap and effective tank-hunter and infantry support weapon, and it was designed around an APFSDS projectile having a muzzle velocity of 1620 metres/second. The sub-projectile is capable of defeating the NATO single medium plate target at a range of 2 km.

Having got this weapon into a workable state on vehicles, IMI then turned to the idea of placing it on a wheeled mounting, using an old British 6-pounder gun carriage as a test-bed. Having thus proved that the idea was feasible, work has since continued on perfecting a very light and simple carriage with folding trail legs. No details of the weight have been given, perhaps because, so far as we know, the final production design has not yet been settled, but judging by appearance, it is unlikely to weigh over 1000 kg.

In 1985 the French arms consortium GIAT displayed a new 105 mm gun at the biennial Satory exhibition. This calibre is getting away from the 'light' category perhaps, but the weapon itself is light and handy and shows promise. In fact the gun was developed about 20 years ago, but its time was not yet, export sales failed to materialise and the idea was shelved. When the French Army began forming their Rapid Action Force it was thought by GIAT that this would make a useful

lightweight field gun capable of being helicopter-lifted and the idea was revived.

The LTR 105 uses a split-trail carriage made of light alloy, and designed so that as the trail legs are opened a firing platform is lowered, lifting the wheels from the ground. There is a small shield, attached to the elevating mass, and the whole equipment weighs 1250 kg. Firing standard 105 mm HE shells it ranges to 15 km, and with the normal French shaped charge shell it should be capable of defeating 350 mm or more of armour at ranges up to 3 km.

It might be noted that GIAT have also manufactured three models of 90 mm gun for use in armoured vehicles, all of which are relatively light, and it is not beyond the bounds of imagination to see one of these barrels mounted on a lightweight carriage similar to that of the LTR 105 making a useful gun with an all-up weight under 1000 kg.

Also in 1985 the Austrian Noricum company tested a 105 mm gun of their own design. This was little more

---

Below: **The Israeli 60 mm gun: note the fume extractor, which reveals the armoured vehicle origin of the gun.**

Above right: **A model of the Ares remote-controlled 75 mm gun.**

Right: **Guided discarding sabot projectile designed to be fired from a tank gun or other light artillery weapon.**

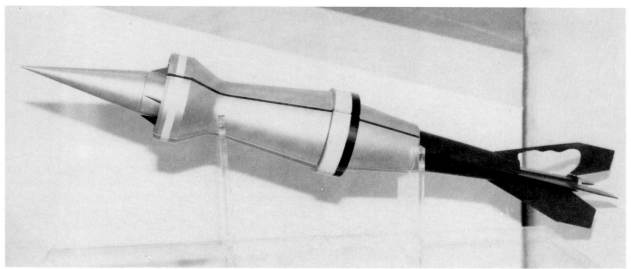

than the well-known 105 mm L7 tank gun placed in a long-recoil mount on a wheeled split-trail carriage, but it makes a very potent anti-tank weapon. It fires all the NATO-standard range of 105 mm tank gun ammunition, and is also capable of firing a special APFSDS projectile developed by Noricum in conjunction with the Hirtenberger ammunition company. At 3600 kg this 'ATG-N-105' is by no means a lightweight, but compressing the undoubted power of the 105 mm L7 gun into a wheeled carriage and still keeping the weight within the moving capacity of six men is nevertheless a clever achievement.

In 1986 the Ares Corporation of America announced a new concept in anti-tank defence, that of a remotely-controlled 75 mm gun. The weapon sits on a conventional wheeled carriage but instead of being attended by a detachment of men is provided with a bore-sighted television camera and a fully automatic magazine. The gun can be emplaced in any suitable spot and the controls for aiming, firing and reloading linked to a distant observer by either cable or digital radio link. The observer sees what the gun's camera sees, and he can thus swing the gun to observe (or may have an independent wide-angle camera for surveillance) and then use the camera to aim and fire the gun. It reloads automatically after each shot until the six-round magazine is empty. At this point, of course, the whole system grinds to a stop until some intrepid soul goes out and reloads the gun's magazine, which might not be a particularly practical exercise in the middle of a battle.

All these weapons were introduced with the tank target uppermost in the designer's mind, and with general support second – although we take leave to doubt if general support is even contemplated in the Ares design. But the inclusion of the helicopter in the list of potential targets makes one wonder how these weapons will respond. Direct shooting is possible, of course, given accurate laser rangefinding, and the high

Above: **The Belgian Mecar 90 mm KEnerga anti-tank gun.**

velocity of this class of weapon means that the helicopter has very little hope of avoiding the projectile as it might a missile. More probably the solution lies in the adoption of guided projectiles; these have been experimentally produced in calibres as small as 40 mm, and as the illustration shows a discarding sabot guided projectile has been developed for tank guns and could equally well be used in wheeled equipments. Given a suitable homing device, it would seem that the helicopter's days are numbered.

The most recent introduction in this field, announced in November 1986, is the Oerlikon Iltis infantry gun, a 25 mm Oerlikon KBB automatic cannon on a lightweight tripod mount fabricated from composite materials. Cannon of this type are not exactly new, and many armies deploy them in the light air defence role, giving them a secondary anti-light armour task as well. But all suffer from the same disability: the weapon is controlled by a gunner sitting behind it with a fairly prominent sight unit, giving the whole affair a high silhouette and inviting destruction.

The Iltis gets around this in a particularly clever manner. The sight fitted to the gun is a TV camera or some other form of electro-optic sensor, and its output is channeled down a fibre-optic cable to a viewing device worn by the gunner on his helmet, suspended in front of his eyes. He therefore no longer needs to sit upright behind the weapon, applying his eye to an optical sight; he can crouch down behind it, well below the axis of the barrel in fact, controlling the aiming by an extension arm and relying upon the image displayed on his mask to aim the weapon. The gun has two 15-shot magazines, one at each side of the receiver; one can be filled with anti-armour ammunition, the other with anti-personnel projectiles or anti-material fragmentation and blast shells, and the gunner can select from which magazine the gun will feed.

It should be stressed that Iltis is not the usual air defence gun with ground capability; its maximum elevation is 45 degrees, which means that as a conventional anti-aircraft weapon it is useless. But this amount of elevation is satisfactory for engaging helicopters hovering over the treeline some 2 km distant, waiting for a shot at an approaching tank. And with a muzzle velocity in the region of 1200 metres/second, a hovering helicopter is going to stand very little chance of survival. The whole weapon, in action, weighs only 240 kg, and it can be carried in individual loads by

Above: **The Austrian Noricum N105 gun is based on the well-distributed 105 mm L7 tank gun, and has a formidable anti-armour capability.**

four men. It can also be mounted in the back of a vehicle or fitted with wheels and towed.

There are, then, a number of guns which appear to be well-suited to the infantry anti-tank and support role. The question remaining to be addressed is that of how to use them. Or, rather, of how to incorporate them into the existing organisations, since any suggestion of adding them to what already exists will bring screams from the overburdened troops.

The demise of the anti-tank gun led to a search for a replacement, and into this gap the missile landed very nicely. Since when it has become an article of faith that the missile is the solution to the tank. And so it is; but not the sole solution. In the first place, while the missile is the answer to the tank it is far more than the answer to minor armour – IFVs, MICVs, APCs and light reconnaissance vehicles. Using a missile to defeat these is like building a gallows merely to wring a chicken's

neck; they can be equally well defeated by solid shot fired from light guns. And since the missile has become the sole solution, its distribution has reached a high level – in order to ensure that there is always a missile where a tank is likely to appear – and thus a grossly expensive business. The price of one light gun and ten rounds of ammunition is probably close to the price of one missile launch post and ten reloads; but after that the price advantage of the gun takes an upward curve, since the gun is capital equipment and the price of one round of gun ammunition is one-fiftieth of that of a missile.

Currently, the drawback to a missile system is the requirement for the operator to keep his attention fixed on the target throughout the missile's flight. Until the shot has been seen to succeed or fail, the operator cannot begin to appraise his next target and take it under engagement. This places a saturation level on the immediate front, governed by the speed at which tanks can be engaged by missiles. The gun, on the other hand, with its far higher velocity, disposes of one shot in a few seconds, after which the gunner is ready to repeat it or look for another target; the saturation level becomes much higher, since more targets can be engaged during the enemy's final run-in. Where a single missile post might be able to engage five targets, a gun should be able to engage twenty.

We are, of course, told that the 'fire-and-forget'

119

The French light 105 mm gun on tow behind an Acmat 1.5-tonne truck. The barrel would normally be depressed and clamped for travelling.

missile will make this calculation obsolete, and that once this missile appears the saturation level will be the same as that for a gun; fire the missile, bless its departure, look for a fresh target. But anyone with experience of military equipment knows that the 'fire-and-forget' missile is going to be vastly more expensive than the second-generation wire-guided weapon, and this, in turn, means that there will be less of them. So there will still be wire-guided missiles in service, if for no better reason than they have been bought and paid for and their total replacement with 'fire-and-forget' will be too expensive to contemplate.

It is, therefore, for argument that as and when the 'fire-and-forget' missile appears in small numbers, some of the wire-guided missiles could be replaced with guns. This would have the two-fold benefit of firstly replacing the missiles with a weapon with faster reaction time, and secondly of saving money which might then go to improve the number of third-generation missiles.

Moreover, we must not be so besotted with the anti-armour war than we overlook the helicopter, since this, in the next few years, is going to become a very serious threat indeed. It might be possible to fly a wire-guided missile against a helicopter, but it would be a fairly dense helicopter pilot who was unable to avoid it for most of the time. The gun projectile, on the other hand, cannot be avoided; the small-calibre weapons with a high rate of fire, such as the Iltis 25 mm cannon, would be formidable, and even the heavier weapons, provided with homing projectiles, would be an extremely serious threat.

Taken together, there is room for thinking that a return to the light gun might show distinct advantages on tomorrow's battlefield.

Overstretch

Geoffrey Manners

Militarists visiting the British Army's prestigious Equipment Exhibition in Aldershot last summer drove past large hoardings advertising the forthcoming Aldershot Army Display, the annual, glossy occasion when the Army shows off its talents. But pasted diagonally across the signs this year was the rueful message from the Army 'Regret Cancelled'. The reason, said the MoD, was 'pressures on manpower as a result of worldwide committments'.

Soon after that embarrassment, General Sir Martin Farndale, commander of the Northern Army Group, speaking to *Jane's Defence Weekly*, warned that NORTHAG's manpower 'was at a minimum safe level'. And even as he was speaking, civil servants and officers in the MoD's Defence Secretariat were looking westwards to the Caicos Islands, a British West Indies dependency in the Caribbean, where a constitutional crisis was rumbling and to which British troops might have to be sent to assist the local authority.

On everyone's lips was the fashionable word 'overstretch' which superficially means having too many jobs in the diary, or not enough men. But it is not that simple. The West Germans are facing up to their forthcoming demographic trough by lengthening their National Service period from 18 to 21 months. Reintroducing National Service is not a cure for the UK's problems, even if politically acceptable. It is the diversity of calls on time and a shortage of units that leads to 'overstretch' rather than a straight shortage of men. The diversity includes maintaining rotations to Northern Ireland, the Falkland Islands (Malvinas), Hong Kong, Belize, Cyprus and in and out of West Germany.

Cancellation of the Display was not a political decision to make a point. It was a command decision brought about by the deployment to Northern Ireland of extra battalions to meet the worsening situation there. A total of 37,000 man hours was involved – 30,000 were saved and 7000 transferred to the Equipment Exhibition. The cancellation occured because of an imbalance between commitments and resources, or 'overstretch'. But the Army was quick to point out that it was an operational commitment it was meeting.

The cancellation just stripped a bit of icing off the cake. From the Army's point of view displays are fine but they are not particularly significant except in terms of public goodwill. It would have been a more serious matter had it had to cancel a major exercise.

It is difficult to define 'overstretch'. One man's overstretch is another man's busy day. Much depends on the competence of the individual or units who claim to be either busy or overstretched. If the politically-imposed committments like Cyprus, Belize and the Falklands (Malvinas) were to disappear and the Army cancelled all displays, and carried out only local-area training, overstretch would disappear at a stroke. But it would bore the pants off the units within days.

So the trick is to achieve a balance between a busy life and overstretch – this could be described as the point at which the individual soldier or the unit collectively feels that it can no longer meet its own professional standards in each of the things it has been called upon to do. Most soldiers or units are content to go on a succession of exercises provided each of those activities can be executed satisfactorily to meet the individual's own standards.

Overstretch starts to impact on a soldier when he feels he is not doing a job properly because he has not the time either to prepare for it or to execute it. At this point a further consideration needs to be taken into account. Wives who aren't motivated militarily in the same way as their husbands feel it keenly if their men are out of bed for too many nights of the year. If that happens the soldier comes under 'overstretch' pressure at home. And the MoD freely admits a soldier abroad can face 'long periods of separation and a disruption of home life'. In BAOR, for instance, the conversation generally gets around to the number of nights the soldier is away from home. He might be on exercise, he might be on a course, he could be in Northern Ireland.

BAOR, which does not like talking about Northern Ireland because of the political embarrassment of not maintaining the full 55,000 designated troops in West Germany, is to take over the United Nations Force roulement task in Cyprus with its non-infantry units. The Army says that the sunny Cyprus posting will be a welcome relief to soldiers after the cold north German plains. And it means less time in Northern Ireland

because the West Belfast battalion commitment will be transferred to the UK. But there is an element of sticking wallpaper over the cracks in this manpower game. The jobs that need to be done in West Germany do not disappear because some men are packed off to Cyprus.

It was the same with the emergency in the Caicos Islands. In some circumstances the MoD, not having one of HM ships to anchor over the horizon, might have deployed the Spearhead Battalion, or at least part of it. After all, it should be able to deploy anywhere in the world – that is its role. But Northern Ireland is a running sore and in the last decade the Spearhead Battalion has, in practice, become a standby for that area only. Take away the Falklands (Malvinas) campaign and not many can remember when the Spearhead Battalion was last operationally deployed.

So the operational consequences of sending men of 3 Queens, an infantry battalion based in Belize, to the Caicos were examined. But that would have increased the pressures on those left behind in Belize. Once again, the wallpaper was nearly unrolled.

The very mention of a firemen's strike, or a dustmen's dispute is sufficient to give the staff at the United Kingdom's land forces' headquarters grey hairs. Military aid to the civil authorities can include assistance with strikes, floods, water provisions and counter-terrorist operations. Some proposed industrial disputes mean soldiers standing by to intercede, and that means training, sometimes in secret, lest their potential involvement inflames a delicate industrial situation.

The ground-launched cruise missile complexes at RAF Greenham Common and Molesworth also have to be guarded and the Army has been, in the past, and no doubt will, in the future, be called on to provide men to protect the sites from the angry women. Now that is a job the Army could do without.

Crisis management or not, the Army has not yet failed to meet an operational commitment. The time has not yet come – though some say it cannot be too far away – when the politicians are told by the Army 'No more. Enough is enough'. Northern Ireland is the obvious case, but they have also never failed minor deployments, like a fistful of soldiers to the Solomon Islands to help with flood relief. Neither have they failed to turn up on time in the UK on operational matters. Army Explosives Ordnance Disposal teams are often called

out to assist the police with clearing devices. Other British Army commitments, world wide, are listed below.

It is the exercises that suffer, after the public relations displays. One exercise was cancelled last year, but that was hardly a serious matter. It would be a relatively easy matter to reduce exercises worldwide. But take away the overseas training trips – and they are needed because of the lack of UK training areas – and recruitment drops, and overstretch rears its head again. A look at the British Army's training programme for 1986-87 shows how attractive it is for the average soldier who wants to get around the world a little.

Every four or five years there is a major exercise to practise the rapid movement of reinforcements to BAOR. In 1984, for instance, some 57,000 troops deployed from the United Kingdom land forces to BAOR during Exercise Lionheart.

Since the Falkland Islands (Malvinas) war in 1982 out-of-area training has assumed a greater importance. Both sea- and air-mounted operations are practised regularly by 5 Airborne Brigade and 3 Commando Brigade Royal Marines.

In the UK there are six principal training areas, 62 training camps, 12 intermediate training areas, six specialist training areas, 93 subsidiary training areas and 74 outdoor range complexes. But these are not enough to meet the needs of the field army and the training organisations, which means that some training must be carried out overseas. In 1986-87 there were 163 overseas exercises planned in 21 countries. These comprised one each in Australia, Holland, New Zealand, Portugal, Spain and Turkey; two each in Brunei, Canada, the Caribbean, France, Hong Kong and Oman; five each in Belgium and Kenya; six in Denmark; 11 in the USA; 13 in Gibraltar; 24 in Cyprus and 67 in BAOR. There were also 104 to be held in the UK.

Then, of course, there is always the unexpected, like the Falklands (Malvinas) war. The unexpected could include going to the assistance of an ally or friendly country under threat and requesting assistance, or where British subjects are at risk with the possibility of evacuation. Troops for such non-NATO out-of-area operations have to be found either from units earmarked for home defence or for NATO reinforcements. A continuous roster of units is maintained in connection with these possible operations with an 'Spearhead' Infantry Battalion Group at 72 hours' notice to move any where in the world. (But inevitably, as mentioned earlier, that means Northern Ireland.) Its lead elements, a company group, are always on 24 hours' notice to move. Additionally, there is the Leading Parachute Battalion Group, which is one of the two in-role Parachute Battalions forming part of 5 Airborne Brigade. In the event of a larger force being required the whole of 5 Airborne Brigade could be deployed, with, if necessary, 3 Commando Brigade of the Royal Marines.

All this commitment comes from the peacetime strength of the UK's land forces of around 150,000 men and women. This number increases to over 200,000 with the mobilisation of reserves.

But at that stage, overstretch is the last thing on anyone's mind.

The British Army used 70,641 men abroad last year, and the deployments were broken up as follows:
- West Germany 55,997, elsewhere in continental Europe 3853
- Gibraltar 771, Cyprus 3177, elsewhere in Mediterranean, Near East and Gulf 238
- Hong Kong 1964, elsewhere in Far East 235
- other locations 4406

Right: **A Milan anti-tank team on a river crossing. Preparations like this proved invaluable to the British during the Falklands (Malvinas) war. Incidentally Milan proved to be a very good but expensive infantry weapon for clearing Argentinian sangars. (***MoD***)**

Below: **Training in Wales – this was one of 104 such exercises held in the UK last year. There were 163 overseas. (***MoD***)**

These figures include loan service personnel. Personnel serving in Northern Ireland on emergency tours of duty but remaining under the command of BAOR are included in West Germany, while personnel serving on emergency tours of duty in other overseas areas, are included in the numbers for that area.

The Army deployments earlier this year and broken down into units, were as follows:

Canada
Training Unit

Belize
1 Armed Recce Troop
1 Field Artillery Battery
1 Engineer Squadron
1 Infantry Battalion
1 Flight AAC

Falkland Islands (Malvinas)
1 Infantry Battalion Group
Supporting arms and services

Northern Ireland
HQ Northern Ireland
2 Brigade HQs
1 Engineer Squadron
6 Resident Infantry Battalions
4 Roulement Infantry Battalions (one may be RM Commando)
2 Squadrons AAC
9 Battalions UDR

United Kingdom
Specialist reinforcement units for NATO
Reinforcements for BAOR
Forces for home defence
1 SAS Regiment

Gibraltar
1 Infantry Battalion
1 Surveillance Troop
Royal Artillery

Cyprus
1 Armoured Recce Squadron
1 Engineer Support Squadron
2 Infantry Battalions
1 Flight AAC

Kenya (Exercise)
Engineer Squadron

Brunei
1 Gurkha Infantry Battalion
1 Flight AAC

Norway (Exercise)
1 Infantry Battalion Group

Berlin
Infantry Brigade

West Germany
1 Corps HQ
3 Armoured Divisions
1 Artillery Division
1 Artillery Brigade

Hong Kong
1 Gurkha Engineer Regiment
5 Infantry Battalions
1 Squadron AAC

Abbreviations:
AAC   Army Air Corps
Recce Reconnaissance
SAS   Special Air Service
UDR   Ulster Defence Regiment
Note: This does not include 662 loan service personnel deployed worldwide.

Training on Chips

Stephen Broadbent

Compared with air forces, armies have been very slow to adopt the microchip and microelectronic technologies within their equipment. Driven by an overpowering need to get as many functions within the space and weight constraints of a military attack aircraft as possible, microelectronics' designers have been forced to develop more and more ability in smaller and smaller circuits, or 'chips'. Army equipment does not place the same severe demands on the designers, and electronics are not as much the driving force in tank or gun development.

This rapid development in the aerospace world has had a key knock-on effect – aircraft are now so complex, and hence so expensive, that air forces often have to limit severely the amount of flying pilots are allowed, not to mention the number of aircraft actually bought. For some years now the limitation in flying has meant that pilots have not been able to undergo anything like the amount of training required to keep them competent in tactics and procedures, so air forces have been seeking effective ways of providing this training, at a cost significantly less than real flying.

But aviation electronics – avionics – are very expensive, because, firstly as systems, they are only produced in relatively small quantities, and secondly, in order to provide the very high level of reliability demanded by the user, under conditions of very high altitude, 'g' loading and vibration and very low temperatures, the electronic circuits have to be of 'state of the art' standard of design and fabrication.

Discount the cost of fuel, and a training mission carried out in a ground-based training system becomes almost as expensive as an aircraft if avionic standard electronic components are used, and there is little point in developing such training aids. However, the development of each successive generation of ever more capable chips has led to previous generations rapidly becoming 'old technology' and relatively cheap to produce in large quantities for the domestic market, where performance demands are far lower than in an aircraft. The chips in the household washing machine or pocket calculator started their development lives, as likely as not, on a military drawing board.

This has provided the answer to the problem of training aids being too expensive – chips of low quality (compared with that required for airborne use) can be used in the benign atmosphere of a classroom trainer, the cost of which is thus dramatically reduced. Suddenly, the advent of the mass-produced, commercial chip has reduced the cost of flying training by perhaps ten-fold, opening up a whole new world of training possibilities, not dependent on, and far, far cheaper, than real flying. The revolution started with full-flight trainers, which some years ago were cleared to train commerical pilots all the way to their licence, and as chips have got ever cheaper, many training systems which are merely an extension of the familiar desk top personal computer, are helping air force personnel achieve better 'on the job' results, whatever their trade.

But the army has been slow to catch on. Traditional methods have held sway, it being considered perhaps that firing a real bullet at a real target is far better training than 'pretending' with a simulator. After all, bullets, or conventional shells don't cost that much, do they? But they do, when added together, and all the wasted bullets soon add up to the cost of a trainer, given today's cheap electronics and powerful software – and, of course, once a trainer is purchased it costs very little to operate until it needs replacing, whereas bullets, shells and fuel are a continual cost, and get more expensive.

At last, then, armies are beginning to adopt electronics-based trainers, and having waited so long, the range of aids which are readily available by relatively simple development from air force systems, is huge. The 'training on chips' revolution is hitting armies fast and hard, and saving vast amounts of money.

There are so many applications for training aids with the current state of electronics technology, that it is impossible to review them all. However, before selecting a sample to indicate the breadth of that range, an examination of 'why training aids' will explain why there are so many varied types.

Apart from the very large cost savings which derive from even the most simple training aid, the reasons for employing one can be summed up in two words: 'effectiveness' and 'motivation'. For some reason young people (who are essentially the largest proportion of those likely to be trained this way) take very eagerly to

electronics, and the ability to learn to fire a gun or drive a tank using a box of electronics in a classroom (or even, with the smaller aids, in the mess or barracks) is very much more appealing than real training in a muddy field or on a freezing, wind-swept range. It is thus generally found that the trainee will voluntarily seek extra practice in 'free time' and will even compete against fellow students on the trainers; all this adds to both effectiveness and motivation when it comes to the real thing, the battle.

And, of course, training on a simulator is far more effective a use of time than is 'real system' training. There is no need to march to the rifle range, or drive for miles from barracks to a tank gunnery range, or wait for training 'slots'; no abandoning of training because of the weather or because of an equipment failure unrelated to the actual training lesson; and no need to assemble, say, a large group of trainees, all in serviceable vehicles or with serviceable equipment: a single trainee can carry out a lesson, with all the many other variables, such as the rest of the tank squadron, being simulated, rather than 'real'. The benefits are endless, given the very high level of similitude now available and, at the end of the day, the bottom line is that the soldier, whether firing, driving or maintaining, will perform far better than before. About the only thing in the army that can't be simulated to provide better training is marching!

At the basic end of the training spectrum are the interactive video systems, which generally take advantage of the rapid access to data permitted by the video disc. Typically, a student would be faced with a conventional colour television monitor, a keyboard and other controls for the desk-top system. Training in maintenance procedures, for example, can be most effectively carried out on such a system – the student is taken through every stage of assembly and break-down of a piece of equipment, such as a rifle, and asked questions by the computer, at each stage.

These questions are set by the tutor, and the answers given are logged in the individual's computer, or they can be relayed to a central area for analysis. Where this type of aid scores over more conventional methods is that the system's program is structured so that incorrect answers can trigger an explanation, a review of the problem, and a re-test, all entirely automatically. Of course, the student can still call up the tutor if he gets really lost, but the program is designed to take the student through the lesson at his own pace until he is

fully competent in the required task, and only then, allows him to move on to the next stage.

Basic mechanical engineering training is well suited to this approach, but it is also useful for the very important task of target recognition training. Moving pictures of tanks or helicopters, for example, can be generated on the screen, with varying conditions of lighting, visibility and terrain. As well as a keyboard, the student may have a steering control and a firing button. As the target moves among natural landscape features, the student has to recognise it as friend or foe, and, to signify the latter, direct a firing marker on to the target and 'fire'. Speed and accuracy of recognition are tested and developed, and eye-hand co-ordination can also be developed and tested on such a system.

The target marker symbol can be refined by making it respond as it would in a real armoured fighting vehicle, so that the student gets an early appreciation of the speed of reaction involved in driving and firing on the move. The sophistication of the training system, as is true throughout the whole range of simulation, can be tailored to suit exactly the customer's needs.

While systems with comprehensive scoring and

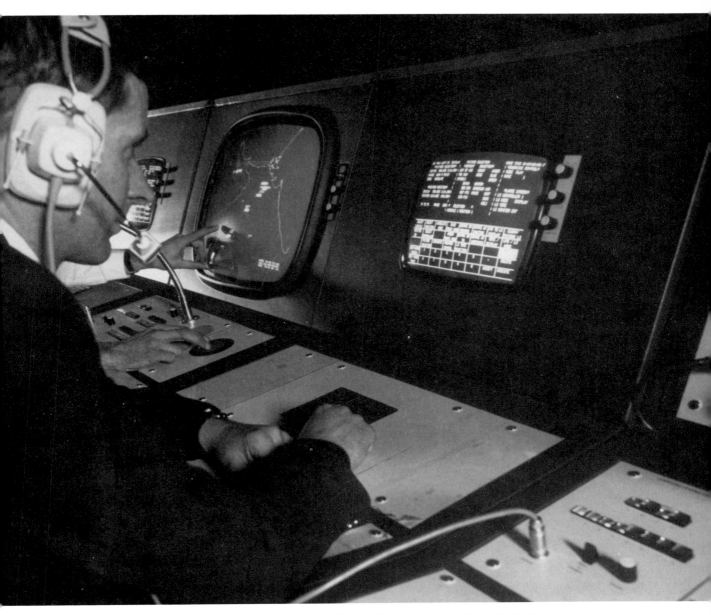

Above: **Solartron computer-based tactical training simulators ensure that command teams and individual operators can be trained and exercised frequently in a realistic environment.** (*Solartron*)

assessment routines would be confined to a formal classroom, the programs are simple enough, and do not necessarily require a video disc facility, so that they can be used without supervsion, and such is the motivation offered by 'computer games' that students are often found using the 'games' on home computers, in a way they would never have thought of doing with conventional manuals.

Operational skills are clearly paramount in an armed force, and any ability a trainee can acquire before using real equipment is obviously going to be beneficial in both operational effectiveness and financial terms. One step up from the desk top interactive systems, a whole range of part task and procedures trainers are evolving, which enable specific tasks to be learnt without involving the whole vehicle or crew. A trainee tank

driver, for example, can sit at a simple simulator, giving him realistic driving controls and a periscope, the view through which responds to the inputs made on the controls. A whole exercise, involving everything from getting the tank underway to driving at high speed in an attacking convoy is possible, with a realistic scene being generated in the periscope, but without the need to involve any other crew member, or any real tank hardware.

Actually firing a gun, missile or rifle is a very expensive event, particularly given the sophistication of today's weaponry, and once again the advent of the 'chip', together with advanced software, is enabling realistic firing to be undertaken, without the need to expend a single real round, and with the added benefit that each shot can be marked immediately, and the performance of each trainee analysed in the associated computer.

Such training aids span the complete spectrum from small arms trainers to simulators in actual tanks. In a typical small arms trainer, ten students can be trained simultaneously, their targets being controlled from, and their performance being monitored at, a single central instructor's position. Each student has a real rifle, modified to 'shoot' a light beam instead of a bullet, and also equipped so as to give realistic recoil and jump actions. Ear defenders, worn by each trainee, include earphones to give a realistic audio effect.

The instructor can select a variety of targets, from a standard static gallery to a moving urban scene, to be displayed on a television monitor placed in front of each student; on firing, the light beam's direction relative to the target is assessed by the in-built computer, and the accuracy of the hit, speed of reaction, etc, calculated. Again, highly motivated training can be offered to a large number of trainees without reliance on weather, range availability or transport to distant sites.

Huge cost saving, compared with training with 'real' rifles is possible, indeed one manufacturer of such equipment claims a saving of almost a quarter in rifle training costs, even allowing for a generous amount of real firing for annual certification, battle training and essential live firing practice. But the real benefit lies in the improved performance of trainees who have, in effect, unlimited 'free' simulated firing training. Similar training aids are available for almost any kind of man-portable weapon, including such missiles as Milan.

But the sharp end of military simulation is in tank and AFV training, where the cost of expending a modern shell is very high, without considering the impracticality of firing real ammunition or missiles from one tank at another vehicle on the move. Practice against stationary targets in well defined safety areas is possible, if expensive, but the only true test of the ability of a crew to react against advancing enemy tanks, until the advent of the simulator, came with real warfare.

Gunnery crew trainers are the first part of a series of systems which can replicate hostile conditions. A full AFV crew can sit in a simulated turret, with all the controls and displays exactly as in real life. Realistic scenes are generated through the sights, including infra-red for night-time training. The crews can operate every function and see the fully realistic effect. A major benefit is that such trainers cn be trailer-mounted and can thus

be taken to and operated at any site with electric power.

The trainer can stay with the battalion, so as to give continuous training at times of deployment, when crews must stay fully sharp. Alternatively, a single trainer can visit various regiments on a rota basis to give periodic training or assessment. Like all computer-based training, such systems can simulate any scenario or any failure, and can have full trainee-analysis and de-brief facilities built in.

While such a 'fixed based' but transportable system can also be configured as a driver procedures trainer, the next step up the ladder in sophistication is the driver simulator, which provides a fully realistic environment for trainee drivers. To give added realism, a full motion system is included, which means that every steering command made by the driver, and every contour of the land is faithfully reproduced, both in the driver's view and in perceived motion of the cockpit.

The view is, of course, again synthetic, and the very latest visual system technologies are used to provide a true-to-life picture, for the better the visual, the more realistic and beneficial is the training. Several other vehicles can move about the scene, either under computer control or 'driven' by the instructor. Indeed, the concept can be taken a step further and several such simulators, not necessarily in the same location, can be used in unison, or as adversaries, with one being the 'commander' and others following orders or practising attacks.

These systems are very sophisticated, both in hardware and software, and also in the visual systems. For example, objects are realistically obscured as they pass behind obstacles in the driver's line of sight – a particularly difficult piece of simulation. These moving simulators are just as complex and technically advanced as the latest aircraft simulators, and can offer realistic training at a fraction of the cost of the real thing.

The US Army has wrapped up this whole concept of sophisticated training in one huge project known as COFT – Conduct Of Fire Training. A total of 270 COFT systems have been ordered, and many are already deployed throughout the US Army's bases at home and in West Germany and Korea.

COFT is used to instruct the gunners and commanders of M1 Abrams, M2 Bradley and M60 vehicles in every aspect of their tasks. The system simply wouldn't be practical without large-scale use of microelectronics, and some measure of the costs of operating the actual vehicles can be gained from the fact that each COFT costs over $2 million.

Below: **The Desk Top Gunnery Simulator (DTGS) accurately simulates the essential parts of an AFV gunner's task and enables both initial and continuation training to be carried out in the classroom. (***Solartron***)**

Right: **Computer-generated images on a typical tank driving simulator. (***Solartron***)**

The standard COFT, which has been developed by the American General Electric company and uses DEC VAX and GE computers, is deployed in four standard-sized shelters, and one or more is assigned to each base where the M1, M2 and M60 AFVs are stationed. There is also a transportable version, the first of which were delivered in 1986 to units of the US Army National Guard.

The four shelters house the computer, briefing/de-briefing facilities, the simulated cockpit and an instructors' station. The basic philosophy is to take students through a programme of tuition and learning at their own speed: they start by firing from a stationary vehicle at a stationary target in good visibility. As proficiency is gained so motion is added to target and platform, and weather and lighting conditions are varied. In all there are 500 steps to full proficiency and the computer can judge whether a particular student needs to repeat a stage or can jump a few. Problems can be identified and the exercise stopped at any time, and, since all events are recorded, any part of a lesson can be replayed, either for analysis or further tuition. In the end the student will be firing from a moving vehicle, with several possible targets, all moving, in poor visibility at night – the 'enemy' can even fire back!

Clearly, such a structured exercise could never be programmed with real vehicles, even if costs were not a factor, but this structured approach leads to one other, very important benefit – all the students, right across all the tank and AFV battalions, are trained, marked and assessed to exactly the same standards determined by a system-wide common computer program. There can be

no favouritism, no hard luck stories because of bad weather or broken equipment; every student gets exactly the same treatment, the army has a listing of each student's performance and capabilities and, apart from saving huge sums of money, knows for sure that its tank crews are very highly trained.

But there is nothing like the real thing for the best training, even when the cost saving and better, more uniform training of these sophisticated simulators are considered. Real driving and firing on real ranges is still

the best, but the cost, and danger, of using live ammunition precludes the ultimate in realism.

This problem is overcome by another series of trainers, applicable to everything from a rifle sight up to a main battle tank, which permit 'shots' to be fired and casualties and hits to be 'scored' in total safety, *and* the reasons for a miss, for example, can be analysed fully after the event.

Such devices rely for their accuracy on the use of an eye-safe laser which is projected out of the rifle barrel instead of a bullet. In larger guns and tanks the computer is small and versatile enough to allow for the difference between the shell's parabolic trajectory and the laser's straight line when pointing the laser, not along the line of a barrel, but at a different elevation to give correct fall of 'shot'. When a target is hit, laser detectors cause a siren to sound, or smoke to be emitted, to indicate the kill; the laser can even cause a vehicle's engine to be immobilised to prevent escape! Only the exercise umpire, equipped with a special 'laser gun', can re-activate the 'dead' and allow them to retire from the field, or re-enter the battle as a new unit, but only after having discussed the reasons for their being hit.

So, from simple rifle practice, all the way to full in-the-field training exercises, the microprocessor and computer technologies are leading to better and better training for every branch of the army.

Above: **Simfire S Series, seen here on a British Army Challenger MBT, duplicates the ballistic characteristics of the main armament so accurately that it can be used for precision gunnery training. (***Solartron***)**

The Burney Guns

Ian V. Hogg

The introduction of a practical recoilless gun into combat is generally attributed to the German parachute troops who descended on Crete in 1941, though there are fragmentary reports of similar weapons having been used by the Soviets in Finland in 1939/40. Subsequent development of recoilless (RCL) guns was undertaken by the Americans, who were able to get 57 mm and 75 mm types into service in the Pacific theatre before the war ended. These two weapons, widely copied since then, are now familiar. What is less well known is the British development of RCL guns, which resulted in six designs before the end of the war. None of them ever reached service status, but they formed the foundation for the successful 120 mm BAT. A brief survey of this British programme will be of interest since it has never appeared in print and at the rate of which records are disappearing, even a short history is valuable.

The development of RCL guns in Britain was largely due to one man, Sir Denistoun Burney (1888–1968). Burney had a varied career; he joined the Royal Navy in his youth and during the First World War invented the paravane mine-clearing apparatus. Having reached the rank of commander he retired in 1920 and from 1922 to 1929 was MP for Uxbridge. He was responsible for the design of the R-100 airship which was overshadowed by the R-101, and was consigned to history after the latter's tragic crash. Burney then designed a streamlined motor car which had some success between 1929 and 1933. During the Second World War he invented gliding bombs and other devices, but his favourite project was his recoilless gun.

He began work on this some time in 1941, by converting a 4-bore duck gun and firing it successfully. He then obtained the interest of the Broadway Trust, a research and development company set up by Beardmore Engineering Co and some others in order to develop weapons. With their co-operation, Burney now developed a 20 mm RCL single-shot gun which he appears to have demonstrated successfully some time in the spring of 1942. This became the standard demonstrator, though there seems to have been an intention to eventually continue work on it and convert it into a fully automatic weapon. The gun weighed 50 lb (22.7 kg) and fired a standard 20 mm shot at 3500 ft/sec (1067 m/sec);

by comparison, the standard Oerlikon automatic 20 mm gun of the period weighed 143 lb (64.9 kg) and fired the same shot at 2800 ft/sec (853 m/sec). The drawback was that the complete round of ammunition weighed 1 lb (454 g) instead of 7 ounces (198 g).

Since the operation of the 20 mm gun was in all respects the model for the later weapons, a description of this will serve as a basis for subsequent changes. The gun consisted of a 20 mm calibre barrel which was screwed into the front of a 'chamber unit' much larger in internal diameter than the barrel. At the rear, this was closed by a reciprocating bolt, similar to the bolt of a rifle. Above and below the bolt aperture were two bell-mouthed jets pointing slightly up and down the axis of the weapon.

The cartridge case was a steel tube, carrying a percussion cap at the rear and with the 20 mm shell crimped into the mouth. The circumference of the tube was drilled with 152 holes each 3/16th inch (4.76 mm) in diameter. The inside of the case was lined by a tube of waxed paper, and inside this was the propelling charge of 7 oz (198 g) of cordite.

The gun was loaded by withdrawing the bolt and inserting the cartridge so that the projectile entered the rear end of the gun barrel and the rear end of the case rested in the mouth of the chamber. The bolt was then closed, the gun shouldered, and fired by a conventional trigger. The cordite charge exploded, and a proportion of the explosive gas drove the projectile up the barrel in the usual manner. The remainder of the gas burst through the paper lining and escaped through the holes in the case wall into the large chamber, and from there out to the open air by means of the two jets. Thus the rush of gas to the rear compensated for the recoil due to the movement of the shot up the bore, and the gun did not recoil.

At this point, we should perhaps be best served by reading Sir Denistoun Burney's own words, written in a paper entitled *Recoilless Lightweight Guns* in May 1943:

The recoilless gun works upon the same general principle, insofar as recoil absorption is concerned as the Davis gun invented during the last war, the similarity, however, ceases with recoil absorption

because as a gun the new principle inherent in this invention gives a 100 per cent increase in efficiency of propulsion of the projectile as compared with either the Davis gun or any standard of orthodox gun.

It is this increase in the efficiency of the gun itself which enables the reduction in weight of the gun to be made, whereas the elimination of the recoil enables the weight of the mounting to be much reduced.

The principle upon which the gun is based is to discharge gases at high speed to the rear at the moment the projectile starts to move, and a perfect balance is obtained between the forces acting on the gun caused by the propulsion of the projectile and that caused by the propulsion of the gases.

To obtain the necessary gas volume, a considerably larger charge of cordite is used than in the normal gun, but owing to the fact that this cordite is burned in a chamber provided with an open nozzle, the pressure/time curve resulting gives a mean pressure of 80 per cent (of the maximum pressure) as compared with a mean pressure of a little over 40 per cent in the orthodox gun.

The result of this high mean pressure is twofold. Firstly, as the maximum pressure for the same performance is only about half that of an orthodox gun, the metal of the gun walls can be thinner, not only because the pressure is but half but because this thinner metal can be utilised at considerably higher efficiency than that of the orthodox gun. The reason for this additional gain in weight reduction is because as the internal pressure increases, so does the efficiency of the outer layers of the thicker gun walls decrease.

Secondly, an increase in the length of gun is of much higher value than in an orthodox gun.

These two advantages enable one of these new type guns firing a specific weight of projectile, at a predetermined velocity, to be reduced to approximately one-fifth of the weight of an orthodox gun giving the same performance.

The elimination of recoil obviously reduces the weight of the mounting to negligible proportions and enables small size types of high performance weapons to be fired from a man's shoulder. For instance, a 3.5-inch gun (90 mm) weighing 55 lb (25 kg) can be fired from the shoulder, or from a lying or kneeling position with comfort, when discharging a 4 lb (1.8 kg) projectile at 800 ft/sec. Again, a 25-pounder designed on these lines is calculated to have a muzzle velocity of 2100 ft/sec (639 m/sec) but to weigh only 750 lb (336 kg) complete with mounting, as against the service 25-pounder which weighs 2 tons 2 cwt (2.13 tonnes) for an 1850 ft/sec (562 m/sec) velocity.

By this time the War Department had become interested in Burney's ideas, and early in 1943 he produced three designs: one for a 3.45-inch (87.6 mm) shoulder gun, one for a 3.7-inch (94 mm) anti-tank gun, and one for a 95 mm field howitzer. All appeared to be equally attractive and each appeared to have its own particular role to play, so it was decided to leave Burney to develop the 3.7-inch and 95 mm weapons, while the design of the 3.45-inch was taken over by CEAD (chief engineer, armament design) for completion.

Shortly after this various suggestions were being canvassed for a weapon capable of demolishing concrete obstacles at short range – the defences of Fortress Europe were envisaged – and Burney responded with the design of a 7.2-inch (183 mm) RCL gun. Finally, in 1944, he put forward a rather ambitious idea for an RCL 8-inch (203 mm) gun of remarkable power. It will be convenient to consider these various designs in turn.

The 3.45-inch gun developed by CEAD became known as the P1 model, and it diverged from Burney's design in one important particular. CEAD had obviously been impressed by the German 75 mm RCL gun, and abandoning Burney's perforated cartridge case he developed a case with a solid wall but with a corrugated brass base which blew out under pressure and vented into a single jet mounted on the breech block. The percussion primer was carried in the centre of the blow-out disc by a three-legged 'spider', and a central firing mechanism was similarly mounted on the breech block. The breech hinged down to open and was locked by an interrupted collar which engaged with lugs on the outside of the chamber. The gun was 67 inches (170.2 cm) long, weighed 55 lb (25 kg), and fired a shaped charge projectile weighing 4.33 lb (1.96 kg) at a velocity of 900 ft/sec (274 m/sec). Under test, seven shots fired at 500 yards (457 m) range fell into a rectangle 42 × 33 inches (107 × 84 cm).

The only drawback to this weapon, as it eventually transpired, was the severely conical shape of the cartridge case, necessitated by the diameter of the shell at one end and the optimum diameter of the blow-out base at the other. In the long run this proved too difficult to manufacture, and CEAD had to change his design.

Before that, though, early in 1944, Burney, dissatisfied with the P1 gun, had designed the Mark 1 model, which used his own design of perforated case, had four jets surrounding the breech, and was slightly heavier. He also changed the projectile for one of his own design, the 'wall-buster' shell.

Above: **Breech end of the 3.7-in RCL gun.**

Right: **Another rear-end view of the 3.7-in RCL gun, with the breech open.**

Among the several advantages which Burney claimed for his gun design was that of the reduced maximum pressure; this, he claimed, reduced the acceleration forces on the shell and thus allowed him to develop a longer shell of greater capacity. His 'wall-buster' was a thin steel tube with a sharp point, carrying inside it a bag made of woven wire mesh and filled with PE2 plastic explosive. At the rear end was a percussion base fuze. On firing this at a hard target, the outer casing split on impact, and the wire mesh bag deformed and stuck against the target, the explosive then being detonated by the base fuze. This set up shock in the target structure, and when tested against concrete it showed a remarkable ability to blow lumps off the inner side of the target and also break any reinforcing rods buried in the concrete. From then on, 'wall-buster' shells became the standard projectile for all the Burney guns.

The 3.7-inch gun was designed to be capable of being carried by two men or pulled on a light two-wheeled carriage. The barrel could be separated from the chamber section, each component weighing about 100 lb (45.4 kg) and thus capable (in theory) of being carried by one man. There were two jets, one at each side of the screw breech, and the whole weapon, when assembled, was 95 inches (241 cm) long. It fired a 22 lb (10 kg) 'wall-buster' shell at 1000 ft/sec (305m/sec) and could also fire the service 25 lb (11.3 kg) 95 mm

howitzer shell at about 900 ft/sec (274 m/sec). The carriage was of light alloy and weighed only 40 lbs (18 kg). Like all Burney carriages, it reversed the usual order of things in that the trail extended forward underneath the barrel, so as to support the weight; the trail of an orthodox gun extends behind the barrel in order to resist the overturning moment due to the recoil, but with no recoil there was no call for this arrangement, and all the Burney carriage did was keep the gun off the ground in the most convenient manner.

It seems that the 3.7 was designed with two jets, but experience with trial models showed that this was not an efficient design, since the gas from the 5 lb (2.27 kg) propelling charge soon eroded the jet throats and the gun began to 'recoil' forwards since too much gas was getting through. The design was therefore changed to have six smaller jets.

The 95 mm RCL field howitzer was planned to be a powerful weapon capable of taking its place in the divisional artillery. The barrel was 95 inches long and

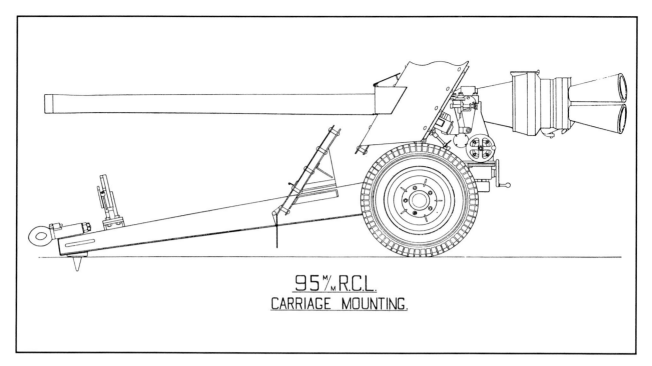

95 ⁿ/ₘ R.C.L.
CARRIAGE MOUNTING.

Above: **Burney's drawing of the 95 mm RCL field howitzer.**

was fitted to a chamber carrying a vertical sliding block breech mechanism with a single jet on either side. It was designed to accept the standard 95 mm infantry howitzer shell and to fire three different charges, the shell and cartridge being loaded separately. This would permit muzzle velocities of 500, 810 and 1070 ft/sec, (152, 247 and 326 m/sec), with an additional 'super charge' giving 1500 ft/sec (457 m/sec). The maximum range would be 10,700 yards (9784 m).

As a result of firing trials with this gun, the chamber was redesigned to give a greater capacity, and four jets were fitted to the breech. This, it was anticipated, would improve the range by about 10 per cent. The complete gun weighed 7½ cwt (380 kg), and it was mounted on a carriage capable of allowing 35 degrees of elevation. This, like that of the 3.7-inch gun, was two-wheeled with a single trail leg beneath the barrel, but it also carried a substantial shield which accounted for almost 600 lbs (272 kg) of the weight. The carriage itself weighed 14 cwt (711 kg), so that the entire equipment in firing order weighed just over one ton (1.02 tonnes). Compared with the orthodox 25-pounder gun's 2 tons 2 cwt (2.13 tonnes) this was a substantial saving, even though the 95 mm could not match the range of the orthodox gun.

It is interesting to note that in mid-1944 Burney had mounted a 95 mm RCL on to the rear of a jeep, antedating the now common method of carrying an RCL gun by several years.

The 7.2-inch RCL gun was designed, as we have said, with the attack of German fortifications in mind. It used a screw breech, had four jets, and employed bag-charge ammunition. The projectile as a massive 'wall-buster' shell weighing 120 lb (54.4 kg) which was fired at 1780 ft/sec (543 m/sec). The carriage was similar to that of the 95 mm but somewhat heavier, and allowed the gun an elevation of 45 degrees, giving it a maximum range of 7000 yards (6400 m).

A second model of the 7.2 was developed after the first had been tested; the changes were largely in manufacturing details, though the chamber was enlarged. A new 135 lb (61.2 kg) 'wall-buster' shell was developed, and this could be fired at 1350 ft/sec (412 m/sec). The entire equipment weighed 32 cwt (1.63 tonnes).

Finally came the 8-inch RCL mobile gun/howitzer, which was put forward in mid-1944. The object was to develop a weapon that would combine the potential of the 7.2-inch howitzer, the American 8-inch (203 mm) gun and the British 12-inch (305 mm) howitzer. In Burney's words, 'That is to say that one unit of the new design has to be of approximately the same weight as the lightest of the three, have the same mobility as the most mobile of the three, to have a greater range than the longest range of the three, and fire a projectile of the same explosive content as the heaviest projectile fired by any of the three'. An ambitious aim.

What made it probable, if not possible, was the ability of a Burney RCL gun to fire projectiles of different weights, with different charges of course, and still have no recoil. It would therefore be designed to fire the standard 200 lb (90.7 kg) 8-inch HE shell; a special

240 lb (109 kg) discarding sabot shell, to compete with the American 8-inch gun for range; and a 520 lb (236 kg) heavy HE shell to compete with the 12-inch howitzer for weight of explosive fired. As calculated, the Burney 8-inch would achieve a maximum range of 36,000 yards (32,920 m) firing the 240 lb shell, thus outranging the American gun by some 2000 yards.

In order to make the design economic, as much of the mounting as possible was to be built from existing components. Thus the wheels and hubs of the British 7.2-inch howitzer, the front axle and wheels of the 40 mm Bofors anti-aircraft gun, the traversing racer and rollers of the 3.7-inch AA gun, the 25 pounder gun sight and the breech mechanism of the 7.2-inch howitzer were all incorporated into the design.

The gun was very unorthodox indeed. The barrel was 32 ft (9.75 m) long, in order to achieve the velocity and range demanded, but to keep the overall length within the limits imposed by the need to tow it on roads, it was decided to place two chambers alongside the barrel, with their breech blocks facing the muzzle. The rear ends of the chambers connected with a transverse chamber at the rear of the gun. This had a third breech block in its centre, aligned with the barrel, through which the shell could be loaded. Thus loading the gun meant opening the rear breech to load the shell, and opening the two forward breeches and loading a cartridge into each chamber. Each of the two forward breeches carried a firing lock, and complicated safety devices had to be devised to ensure that the gun could not be fired unless all three breeches were closed, and that both locks fired simultaneously.

Alongside the third breech, aligned with the two chambers and pointing to the rear, were the two jets, which were quite substantial. The entire weapon weighed 17½ tons (17.8 tonnes) and was towed by a Scammel tractor.

So much for the designs. Now let us see what happened to them. In November 1943 a 7.2-inch 'wall-buster' shell was fired at a five-foot (1.5 m) thick reinforced concrete wall. Fragments were blown 60 yards (55 m) behind the wall, there was severe bulging at the rear, and the internal reinforcing rods were cut. This gave several people a surprise, and early in 1944 the General Staff announced that henceforth the 'wall-buster' projectile would be the preferred solution for the next infantry anti-tank weapon. This, of course, did the recoilless gun programme a great deal of good, and in May 1944 it was reported that the Burney 95 mm gun was being favoured as a future anti-tank weapon. In August the 7.2 was fired again, this time at 6-inch (152 mm) armour plate. It blew off a 117 lb (53 kg) scab from the rear surface, which buried itself 30 inches (762 mm) into the ground and was estimated to have left the plate at 500 ft/sec (152 m/sec).

By this time, of course, the invasion had taken place, and it had done so without the assistance of the 7.2-inch

---

Below: **The 95 mm RCL during its demonstration in Larkhill, December 1944. It blew up shortly after this picture was taken.**

Burney. The reason given was simply that the enormous back-blast from this weapon had no place on a crowded invasion beach, and the 'Petard' spigot mortar mounted on the AVRE tank was capable of doing all the damage to concrete that was necessary. So the 7.2 was abandoned forthwith. It is believed that two were made, one of which was retained at an experimental range for trials, the other being sent to the School of Artillery where it still remains.

In November 1944 the Deputy Director of artillery informed the Ordnance Board that two 95 mm equipments had been built, and requested that trials be carried out to prove its technical feasibility, and also that user trials be arranged. But no sooner had this been said when the priorities of the RCL programme were re-arranged; the 3.45-inch now had top priority, the 3.7 came second, and the 95 mm was 'to remain in abeyance for the time being'.

Next came the news that the 3.45-inch Pl form had run into problems, and that Burney's Mark 1 was now being built; the trials of the 3.45 which had been arranged were forthwith postponed until the new model was available.

In January 1945 came a setback: one of the two pilot model 95 mm guns had been sent to the School of Artillery for demonstration, and in the course of this the shell had burst prematurely in the bore and completely destroyed the gun. This meant holding up everything until an examination had taken place to determine what had caused the accident. Some time later it was found that the fault was in the fuze fitted to the shell; the gun was cleared of any fault, and the development programme began to move once more. Trials now showed the shell to be unstable; the solution was either to re-rifle the gun or adopt another shell, and the 'wall-buster' designed for the 3.7 was adopted. This meant that the chamber had to be redesigned.

At the same meeting which discussed this, it was disclosed that a new design of 4.7-inch (120 mm) RCL gun was under consideration, intended for the short-range attack of Japanese bunkers or tanks. It was suggested that this should be developed at a lower priority, in case the 95 mm failed to meet its requirements. Eventually, orders were given for the

Left: **The 7.2-in RCL gun: the cylinder lying behind the gun is the 'Wall-buster' shell.**

Below left: **The Burney-designed 4.7-in RCL, which later became the 120 mm BAT. Note that this version had two jets springing from the chamber ahead of the breech, whereas the BAT had a single jet set into the breech block.**

Below: **A model of the Burney 8-inch gun, now in the Royal Artillery Museum at Woolwich.**

Above: **The 3.7-in RCL during its travelling and handling trials at the School of Infantry in 1948.**

Right: **Another picture taken at the School of Infantry, showing how the 3.7-in RCL was carried in a 15 cwt truck.**

manufacture of 12 95 mm guns, with 1200 'wall-buster' shells, and four 4.7-inch guns with 1000 high explosive and 400 'wall-buster' shells. It was also disclosed that 135 3.45-inch guns had been ordered.

In August 1945 the war ended, and the many development programmes then running were all given a closer examination. So far as the recoilless programme was concerned, the first decision was to shelve the approval of the 95 mm gun and thoroughly examine the theory behind the 'squash-head' shell, as the 'wall-buster' was now called. So far as can be ascertained, no changes were made to the manufacturing programmes for the guns, however.

Nothing very much seems to have happened until June 1946, when it was decided that the 95 mm gun had a future as a possible field howitzer for use by airborne artillery batteries. In August, therefore, rough use and travelling trials were organised and proof of the manufactured guns was put in hand.

In the same month the 3.45-inch Mark 1 gun, with four jets, was given official approval for service, although none were ever issued other than for trials. It is doubtful that all the 135 ordered were eventually built, and it is likely that most of those built were scrapped, but several have survived in museums.

In December 1946 came the long-awaited report on comparative firings of the Burney and CEAD designs of 3.45-inch gun. The Burney gave the best results for accuracy, but the Ordnance Board considered that 'neither of these guns represents the best that can be offered within a reasonable time. It is appreciated that troop trials with the 3.45-inch RCL will afford valuable evidence as to the acceptability of the RCL principle by the infantry in this role. But it is considered that further design thought, based upon the experience gained with these two weapons should lead to a (better) design.' The Board then enumerated the ideal features, which included a weight of less than 35 lb (16 kg), simple ammunition, and electric firing.

In April 1947 it was found that the RCL guns undergoing proof were showing expansion of the bore, and that this was probably due to the use of solid steel proof shot. Meanwhile the 3.7-inch guns were undergoing handling and cross-country trials. In December the commandant of the School of Infantry reported favourably on these trials, but was told that it had been decided that the 3.7-inch gun would not now be required. 'A small number will be completed for Ministry of Supply requirements, which will be used for trials to complete the data on the performance of this

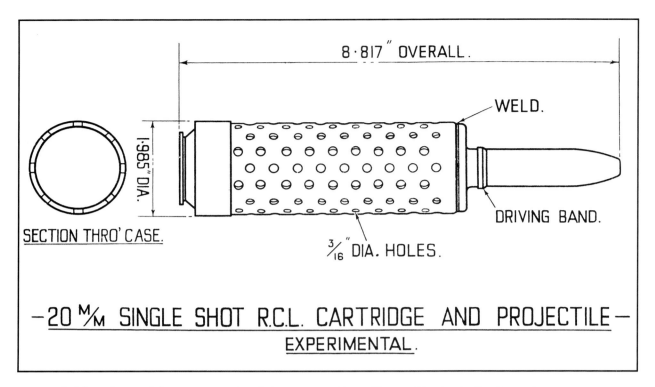

8·817″ OVERALL.

WELD.

1·985″ DIA.

SECTION THRO' CASE.

3/16″ DIA. HOLES.

DRIVING BAND.

—20 ᴹ/ᴍ SINGLE SHOT R.C.L. CARTRIDGE AND PROJECTILE—
EXPERIMENTAL.

weapon.' After these trials were completed, it seems likely that the guns were scrapped; none are known to exist today.

December 1947 saw the formal approval and immediate obsoletion of the 3.45-inch RCL Mark 2; no details of this gun were given in the approval, and it is probable that it was much the same as the Mark 1 but with some design improvements. At the same time the Mark 1 gun was declared obsolete, thus removing both of them from notional service.

At the end of 1947 the development contracts of Broadway Trust Company expired, and the Trust was disbanded. This took Sir Denistoun Burney out of the direct path of development, which left him with an almost-built 8-inch (203 mm) gun on his hands. He had been quietly pursuing this design in the post-war years but the Army had shown no enthusiasm and there had been no official backing for the gun, or any programme of trials arranged. Nevertheless, some time in 1948 he applied to the Army for permission to take it to an experimental range and fire it at his own expense. He did so, but the first shot blew up the gun and wrecked it beyond repair. The project was abandoned forthwith, but in order to extract something of value the Ordnance Board ordered an investigation into the accident to discover what had caused it. It was 1958 before the report finally appeared, and it showed that it was entirely due to the multiple-breech and double-chamber design. Poor ignition of the propelling charges by one of the firing locks had caused the cordite to smoulder, leading to a build-up of high pressure explosive gas within the chambers and gun breech area.

Above: **The cartridge for the first 20 mm Burney experimental gun.**

Right: **Cartridge for the CEAD 3.45-in RCL gun, which used a conical case with a corrugated blow-out disc in the base. The shell is a shaped charge.**

This gas then detonated and wrecked the gun. The design was absolved of blame, the fault lying in the ignition system, but it was recommended that 'multiple firing systems are not to be perpetuated in service'.

Finally, in 1949, came instructions that the design of the 3.45-inch gun was to be completed and then 'shelved against a future demand', and the remaining designs were to be abandoned. In view of the fact that both marks had been made obsolete two years before, it can only be assumed that there had been some improved design on the drawing board which was now being gracefully cleared out of the way. By this time CEAD (or RARDE as it had become) were well ahead on their 4.7-inch RCL design, which was to appear in the early 1950s as the 120 mm BAT (battalion anti-tank) gun. This used a different principle, that of the blow-out base, to Burney's designs and it was the first British RCL gun to achieve service adoption. It was probably also the last.

That, then, was the end of the Burney guns; seven years of work with very little to show for it. What went wrong? There had been some minor problems along the way; at one stage the Ordnance Board, in commenting

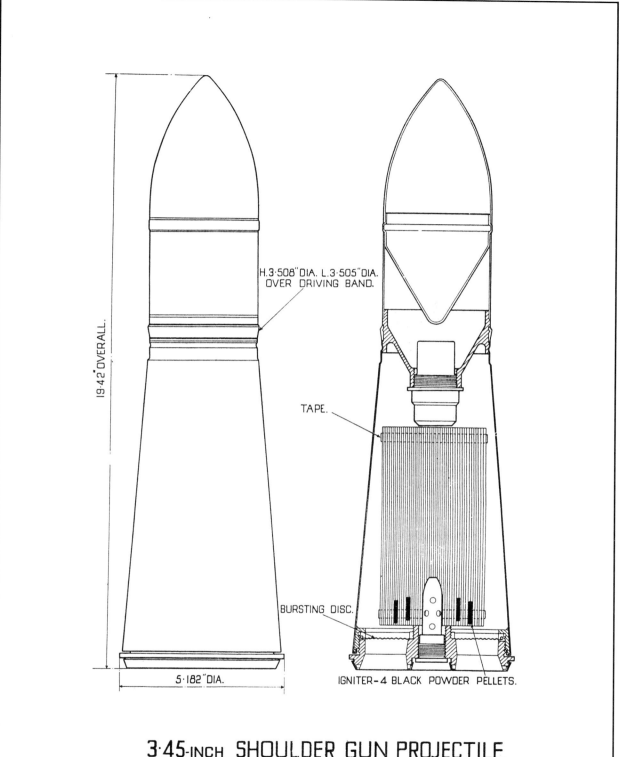

H.3·508″DIA. L.3·505″DIA.
OVER DRIVING BAND.

19·42″ OVERALL.

TAPE.

BURSTING DISC.

IGNITER-4 BLACK POWDER PELLETS.

5·182″DIA.

3·45-inch SHOULDER GUN PROJECTILE.

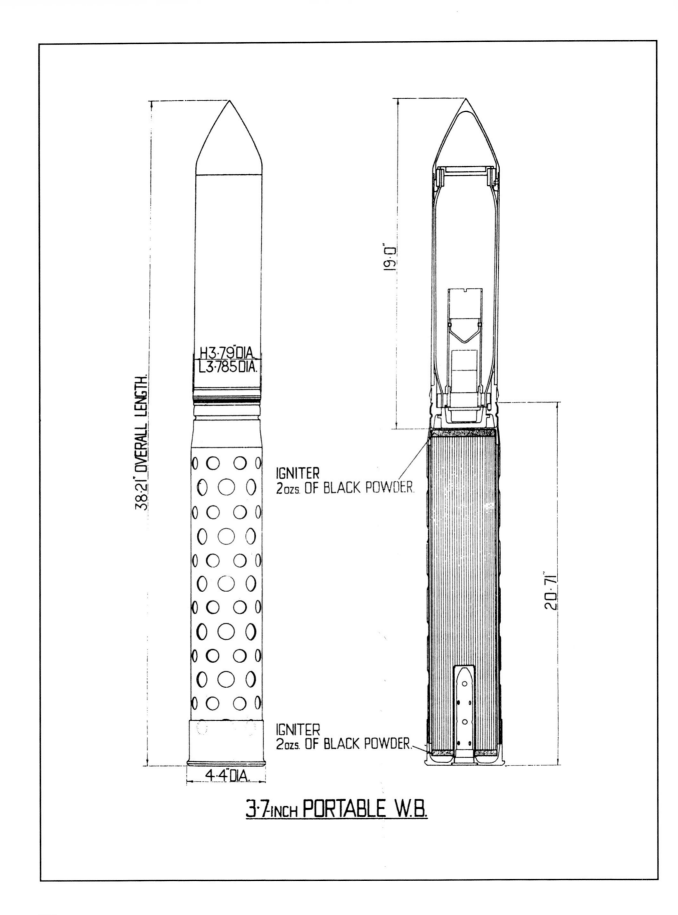

38·21" OVERALL LENGTH.

H3·79" DIA.
L3·785 DIA.

IGNITER
2 ozs. OF BLACK POWDER.

IGNITER
2 ozs. OF BLACK POWDER.

4·4" DIA.

19·0"

20·71"

3·7-INCH PORTABLE W.B.

Left: **The archetypal Burney round: a 'Wall-buster' shell attached to a perforated cartridge case.**

on a future design of 3.45-inch, pointed out that in view of troubles with the existing model particular attention should be paid to the firing mechanism of any new design, which suggests that some difficulties had been encountered. But there do not seem to have been any major setbacks to the programme. Perhaps, like so many other developments of the time, the end of the war came too soon. From unofficial comments it seems likely that had the war in the Far East continued into 1946, as was anticipated, then certainly the 3.45-inch and probably some 3.7-inch would have been sent out for service assessment in combat, just as the Americans did with their 57 mm and 75 mm models. Moreover there do seem to have been periodic changes of heart over the matter of priorities, as if the General Staff were finding it difficult to assess exactly where these weapons might fit into the future army. As it was, the programme appears to have slowed down when the war in Europe ended and lost momentum completely when the Japanese war ended. But although Burney's guns never reached service, his work certainly showed a profit. In the first place it was his early work which set CEAD and RARDE on the road which eventually produced the 120 mm BAT. And, perhaps more important than that, it was Burney's 'wall-buster' shell which formed the basis of the development which led to the adoption of the 'squash-head' shell. This, really, was a 'wall-buster' without the internal mesh bag and with a few other design improvements, but it was essentially Burney's shell, as was the original base fuze. As with so many armament developments, it wasn't the big idea which proved to be the winner, it was one of the minor accessories which eventually overshadowed the rest. So Sir Denistoun Burney ended up with some credit after all.

100 Years Ago

Ian V. Hogg

1886 was a milestone year in weapons' technology, for it saw the invention of a smokeless powder to replace gunpowder in rifled small arms. This was 'Poudre B', invented by Vielle, a French chemist, and named for General Boulanger, the French Minister for War. Poudre B was a nitro-cellulose derived by treating cotton with mixed acids; by modern standards it was somewhat unstable, but this fault did not make itself apparent until it was adopted for artillery cartridges some years later. The advantages derived from a smokeless powder were principally that it contained more power in a smaller bulk that did gunpowder, gave much less fouling in the weapon after firing, was more resistant to damp, and, of course, was smokeless. This latter is a comparative term; it did generate some smoke, but in comparison to gunpowder it could be considered smokeless.

Stemming from these advantages it became possible to reduce the calibre of rifles. That such reduction would bring ballistic advantages had been appreciated for several years, but so long as it was necessary to use bulky charges of gunpowder to develop the required velocities, there seemed no way to reap any benefit from a reduction in calibre. But with Poudre B in their ammunition, the French were able to reduce their service calibre to 8 mm and to adopt the Lebel Modèle 1886 magazine rifle as their service weapon. The Lebel was a bolt action rifle with a tubular magazine beneath the barrel which held eight cartridges.

Small calibre was one aim of the rifle designer of the 1880s; magazine loading was the other, and several systems were undergoing trials during 1886. In Austria, the Mannlicher M1886 rifle was issued in that year and was the first to introduce the clip loading system and box magazine into a production weapon. The Mannlicher used a straight-pull bolt, one in which there is no rotation. The firer grasps the bolt handle and pulls straight back; this pulls the striker back and unlocks a hinged locking block beneath the bolt, so that the pulling movement now draws the bolt open. The bolt is pushed back, picking a cartridge from the magazine as it moves, and the final movement causes the hinged locking block to rise and lock the bolt securely closed. The ammunition was supplied in clips of five rounds; after opening the bolt, so as to expose the top of the box magazine, the entire clip was dropped into the magazine and the bolt then closed. Spring-loaded levers in the magazine forced the cartridge up, between the walls of the clip, so that the forward movement of the bolt stripped the top cartridge out and into the chamber. After the last round in the clip had been loaded, the empty clip fell out of the magazine through a hole in the bottom. The clip was prevented from rising by a spring catch, but this could be depressed to permit withdrawing a loaded or partly-loaded clip, through the open boltway, if desired.

The clip system has one drawback; once the clip is in place, the ammunition in it must be fired or the clip removed. It cannot be 'topped up' by adding loose cartridges, as it can in the charger-loaded rifle. Moreover, in the system designed by von Mannlicher, the hole in the bottom of the magazine, to permit the clip to fall clear when empty, was also a hole through which dirt could enter the rifle action. Nevertheless, clip-loading was fast and reliable, and it remained in service until well after World War II in various forms; perhaps the best known clip loader was the US M1 Garand rifle.

The advent of bolt-action rifles led a number of inventors to contemplate adapting the same mechanism to pistols, and this, in turn, led to a short period in which the aberrant 'mechanical repeating pistol' was vigorously promoted. There were several designs put forward, almost all from Austria or Germany, and one or two even managed to get into production. The general principle of operation was similar: a reciprocating bolt was driven back and forth by a lever operated by the firer's finger. Pushing the lever forward (by means of a ring on the bottom of the lever) opened the bolt; pulling it back closed the bolt and pushed a cartridge into the breech from a magazine, cocking the firing pin as it did so. The final movement of the lever either released the firing pin or brought the firer's finger into contact with a separate trigger which he then pressed to fire.

The theory was impeccable, but the practice depended upon the mechanism being perfectly adjusted and well lubricated and upon the ammunition being of perfect dimensions. All these were doubtless present with a new pistol, being fired immediately after cleaning and adjustment, but the human finger is not well adapted to a pushing movement when crooked, and fouling, dry surfaces and slightly oversize cartridges would soon lead to a demand for a degree of effort not easily produced. The mechanical repeater had a hard struggle to compete against the double-action revolver, and as soon as the automatic pistol appeared on the horizon, it rapidly vanished from the scene.

List of Changes Paragraph 5008, approved 7 April 1885, introduced the first 'quick firing' gun into British service. As with so many 'firsts' it was originally designed for Naval service, as an anti-torpedo boat gun, but was soon taken into coastal artillery for the close defence of harbours. 'Quick firing' – which almost immediately became abbreviated to 'QF' – was the British terminology which signified the use of a fixed round of ammunition with a brass cartridge case, allied to a weapon with a quick-acting breech mechanism. In the case of the 'Ordnance quick-firing Hotchkiss, 6-pounder Mark I', the breech was closed by a vertically-sliding wedge, and the breech block contained a simple percussion firing pin which struck a cap pressed into the cartridge case base. The Hotchkiss was followed, in July 1885, by the Nordenfelt 6-pounder QF gun which differed principally in using a two-part block and wedge breech mechanism. These two guns, of 2.244-inch (57 mm) calibre, were the progenitors of a long line of similar weapons which ended with the 'Twin Six' two-barrelled coastal defence gun which so ably defended Malta in 1942, and the 6-pounder anti-tank gun which survived into the 1950s as the standard infantry anti-tank gun.

Once the quick-firing principle had appeared, there was no delay in seeking to apply it elsewhere: Minute 11090 of the Ordnance Commmittee, 15 November 1886:

> The Director of Artillery requests the Committee to take up the question of fixed ammunition for breech-loading field guns with as little delay as possible. To enable an early trial to be made, two of the Experimental BL guns and limbers can be adapted to this nature of ammunition.

However, it was 1904 before a QF field gun firing fixed ammunition made an appearance in service.

1886 also saw the approval of the first of a long line of heavy artillery, the 9.2-inch (234 mm) gun Mark I. It was 255.8 inches (6.5 m) long, was rifled with 37 grooves which increased in twist from one turn in 118 calibres at the breech to one turn in 35 calibres at the muzzle, and weighed just over 21 tons complete with its screw breech mechanism. Originally approved for Naval service, the 9.2-inch gun was very soon adapted to coastal defence, in which service it remained until 1956, though the final

models (Mark 10) were rather more powerful than the original. In addition it was railway-mounted during the First World War. Although the last 9.2-inch guns were officially declared obsolete in 1956, when British coastal artillery was abandoned, the fact remains that there is still one serviceable 9.2-inch coast gun emplaced on British territory and regularly exercised, albeit without firing. This is the gun in O'Hara's Battery on Gibraltar, carefully maintained in working order as a piece of regimental tradition by the gunners of the Gibraltar Regiment. Other 9.2s, once in British forts, still protect the Portuguese, Turkish and Norwegian coastlines.

Having got the 9.2-inch gun available, the School of Gunnery at Shoeburyness decided to celebrate the Jubilee of Queen Victoria in 1887 in a practical manner: they would raise up the experimental 9.2-inch gun to 45 degrees elevation and see just how far it would shoot. Hitherto maximum range had been of academic interest only, since fire control was strictly line-of-sight and sights were of the blade foresight and vee-backsight variety, none of which were conducive to long-range shooting. But the spirit of scientific enquiry was abroad, fire control was improving, and so it was decided to see what the new 9.2 could do. In the event the problems of devising some sort of mounting to accommodate a 45 degree angle of elevation, and of obtaining the necessary clear range took some time to overcome and it was not until July 1888 that the firing actually took place.

But before performing the 'Jubilee Shot' as it came to be known, the School invited various ballistic experts to forecast what the result would be. Ten experts submitted their calculations for the range and time of flight to be anticipated for a quoted muzzle velocity at 30, 35, 40 and 45 degrees elevation. Their forecasts for 40 degrees ranged from 12,500 to 20,024 yards, but for 45 degrees they were rather closer together, offering solutions between 20,650 and 21,900 yards. All backed their fancy with reams of calculations and formulae.

The results were that at 40 degrees elevation the shot landed 21,203 yards from the gun, and at 45 degrees it landed 21,800 yards away. Only one estimate in the 40-degree group was anywhere close to the real result, at 20,024, but Quarter-Master Hadcock forecast 21,886 for the 45-degree shot, no more than 86 yards out, which was quite a creditable piece of calculation.

What makes amusing reading is the observations of some of the forecasters when they tried to make their calculations fit the observed performance of the gun. Mr Bashforth, professor of mathematics and ballistics at the Royal Military Academy was rather more upset than most: 'He expressed himself satisfied as to the

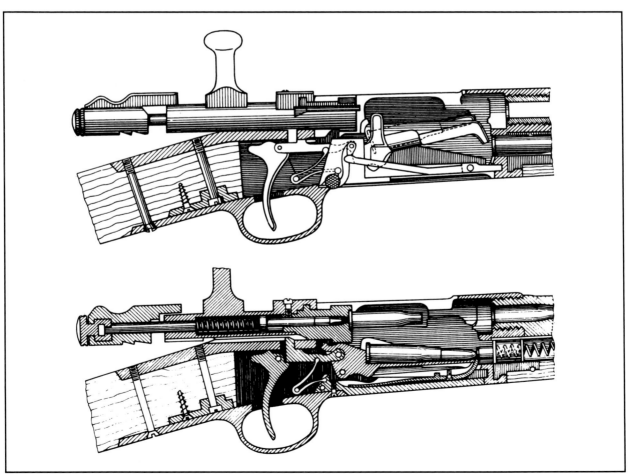

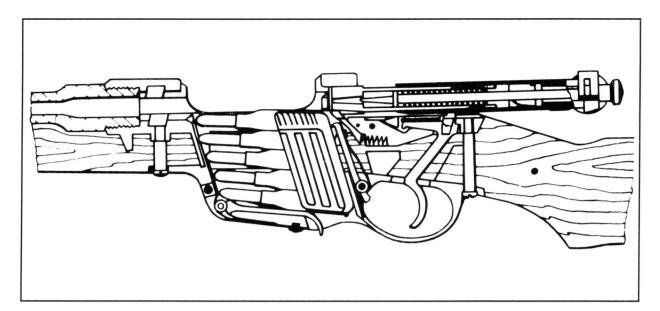

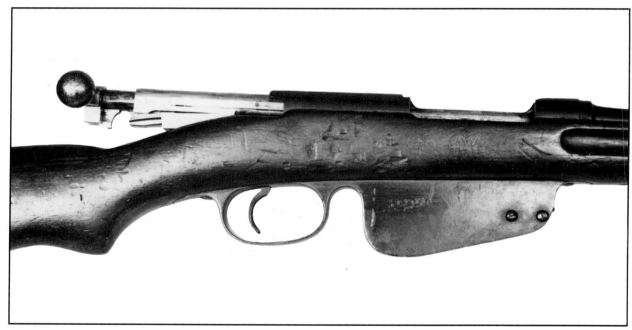

correctness of his tables, but professed himself unable, at present, to explain the actual ranges being 1500 yards in excess of those calculated by him, he did not think that "vertical drift" and "jump" were sufficient of themselves to account for it, and suggested the possibility of the ranges being wrongly measured.' Alas, the reconciliation of theory to practice is something which still plagues scientists to this day.

In spite of the growing number of breech-loading guns being developed, rifled muzzle-loading guns were still being put into service. The *Proceedings of the Royal Artillery Institution*, Vol XIV contains a fascinating short account of the manhandling of two 38-ton 12.5-inch (318 mm) RML guns from the Princes Dock, Bombay, via the Gun Carriage Factory near Vassoon Dock to their emplacements at Colaba Point Battery. The movement began on 11 January 1886 and was performed by placing the guns on to railway trucks specially built for the job and then laying a short length of track in the required direction. The trucks and guns (a total of some 92 tons) were then pulled by 66 men with ropes until they reached the end of the sixteen pieces of track. Then the thirteen lengths behind the two trucks were taken up, carried around, and relaid in the front. The trucks were then pulled forward and the performance repeated. The whole move, covering 2513 yards (2297 m), took six days, after which the guns were manhandled off the trucks, pushed into the battery on rollers, and placed on their mountings by means of sheer-legs and tackle, another week's work.

The British Army made a major reorganisational step on New Years' Day 1887 when it decreed that henceforth fuzes would be identified by numbers, rather than by descriptive names. Thus the 'Fuze, Time, Diaphragm Shrapnel' became the 'Fuze Time No 33'. In the hope of establishing a coherent identification system percussion fuzes were numbered in the 1-20 range, rocket fuzes in the 20-30, time fuzes 30-50 and time and concussion (as they were then known) in the 50s. By the time the numbered series finished in the 1960s, replaced by the 'L' series, the highest numbered fuze was in the region of 950 and the attempt to segregate types into recognisable groups had long since vanished.

Above left: **The mechanism of the Mannlicher clip-loader.**

Left: **The Mannlicher with the bolt open, showing the locking strut beneath it.**

Below: **One of the many designs of mechanical repeater was this pistol by Schulhof of Vienna. The action is fairly easily understood.**

There has never been any shortage of inventors anxious to demonstrate that the entire science of gunnery can be reformed overnight by the adoption of their invention. In 1887 it was the turn of Colonel Hope, VC, who offered a gun built in one piece (somewhat revolutionary for those days) for which he made several extraordinary claims of power and range. In offering it for test he stipulated that 'no official of the Ordnance Department or representative of Elswick is allowed to see it or to have anything whatever to do with it', a caveat which frequently appears in inventor's demands.

Hope was given his chance in November 1887, firing a 2.5-inch gun of his own design. After a first shot at low charge, which was successful, the report (Minute 13963 of the Ordnance Committee) goes on:-

> . . . Colonel Hope then loaded the cartridge and was entreated by the bystanders to proceed cautiously and by degrees, or at least to fire the charge by electricity. He entirely declined to do either and, having placed the spectators under cover of some earthworks, he pulled the lanyard. When the discharge took place the breech block was blown entirely off; a piece of steel flew half a mile up into the air narrowly missing Colonel Hope, and the entire gun was lifted about 15 feet and turned a somersault . . .

Back to the drawing board, I suppose.

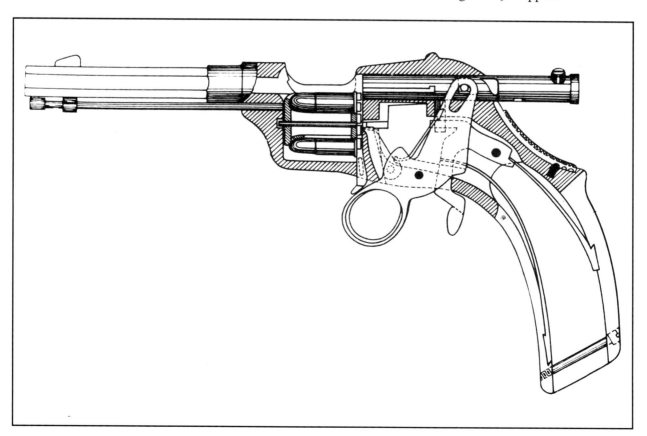

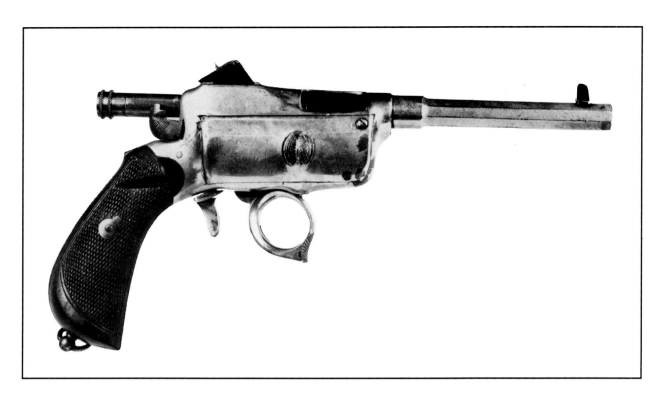

Above left: **Another Austrian mechanical repeater, the Reiger, with the operating lever forward and the bolt open and protruding from the rear of the receiver. The sideplate conceals a rotary magazine.**

Above: **Maintenance on the highly-polished breech of the 9.2-inch gun of O'Hara's Battery, Gibraltar.**

Left: **The Jubilee Shot. How the 9.2-inch gun was mounted so as to achieve 45 degrees for the maximum range. Examination of the original under a magnifying glass reveals that the barrel was lashed to a huge baulk of timber by several turns of rope and the timber then lashed to the recoiling portion of the carriage!**

167